Teaching Today's Youth

—The Challenge and the Victory

Mark A. Simone
and
Kathy J. Simone

ACCENT PUBLICATIONS
Colorado Springs, Colorado

Accent Publications
4050 Lee Vance View
P.O. Box 36640
Colorado Springs, CO, 80936

Library of Congress Catalog Card Number 96-85434

ISBN 0-89636-329-5

Contents

Dedication

We wish to dedicate this book to the memory of our grandparents and in honor of our own parents.

Each of these dear people has touched our lives in many profound ways, influencing our lives through their faithful examples and uncompromising love. We are a product of their prayers, their wisdom, and their time.

We also dedicate our work to our four children: Daniel, the artist, Lindsey, the musician, Erin, the performer, and Nicholas, the naturalist.

May God work through each of you His glory and gifts.

1 The Challenge —and The Adventure

Mark's grandfather used to amaze him with his stories. Grandpa was born in the late 1800s and would talk of the changes he had seen. He remembered life before the automobile, both World Wars, and the Great Depression. He recollected the coming of radio and television. He would talk about farming by hand and life without modern conveniences. Mark loved hearing him talk of Haley's Comet and the fear that swept through the country causing some to take their own lives believing that the comet would descend upon them.

Yet, in spite of all the changes, Grandpa somehow remained relevant to current events and issues. He slightly scorned his friends who longed for the "good old days" and never quite fit in with modern life. Grandpa wanted none of that. He believed in life as it came and taught us to make the best of anything that happened.

In reflecting on his childhood days, Grandpa would tell of only being able to travel the distance that a good horse could cover in a day's time. Trains were for the rich and considered a miracle of speed. Communication was by letter and the news media was the local newspaper and telegraph. International travel could take weeks or even months by ship. The world was shared with others through a good story and meals at the dinner table. Young people took on the livelihood of the family through the family business with the business being passed on from parent to children. No one Grandpa knew went on to college; most "graduated" into the world of work after about eighth grade. A very different world, indeed.

Mark respected his grandfather's ability to take the world, with its innumerable changes, and accept it as his own. He would marvel at technology, even though many of the advances were beyond his ability to comprehend completely. He saw life shift from travel by horse or train to landing a man on the moon. What a remarkable time frame in which to live!

We have seen changes in our lifetimes, too. As children we would watch TV only during the day and early evening; programming signed off after the late news. Today, children may select from just under a hundred channels almost around the clock.

As children we marveled at the advent of the calculator. Now we write these words at a computer with technological advances not available to those administering our nation's space program only a decade ago. In a year, this computer will be obsolete.

Life is every bit as different for today's teenagers as it was for Grandpa and for us. They, too, see changes in technology requiring frequent adjustments of their world view.

In the 1950s, teachers complained about the youth of that decade by expressing dismay over gum chewing in class and loud talking in the hallways. Today's teachers complain of violence to themselves in the classroom and the fear that students bring weapons into the school. Teachers in the 1950s would never have believed that schools in the 1990s would need to install metal detectors to monitor the knives or guns students may attempt to sneak into schools.

In the midst of all of these changes, we, as Christian teachers, volunteers, or youth leaders, have been commissioned to communicate the timeless faith in the gospel of Jesus Christ to this generation of young people. Let's meet a few of today's teenagers.

Meet Claire

Claire is fairly average as teenagers go. She is a good student. She has several friends and loves her cat. She attends a large public school in the Midwest. She is interested in her world and hopes to be a United Nations translator someday in Spanish. She enjoys music, talking about boys, and never misses a meeting of her youth group at First Baptist. She is strong in her faith and takes pride in the fact that she never "makes waves," or causes disturbances. Claire knows that most people don't notice her, but that doesn't bother her much. On her high school jacket she wears a pin that states, "My boss is a Jewish Carpenter." She sings in the church choir and looks forward to church summer camp. Tonight she plans to finish reading the book of James, her favorite book in the New Testament.

Meet Thom

Across the continent, in a large auditorium, Thom is also reading from the book of James in his youth group's Bible study. Almost 200 kids are in his weekly study. He likes the Bible, but, if the truth be known, he really participates because he loves the chance to hang around with kids his age.

Not too long ago he would not have believed that he would ever reach his senior year in high school. He was using drugs, drinking almost every day, and taking risks that now make him shake his head in amazement. He still wears his black leather motorcycle jacket and his hair is still more that of a design than a cut, but more and more he finds himself "putting on the new and putting off the old." For now he is content with his new life and thankful for the team from Grace Church who visited him in the juvenile detention center. If not for them, he would have never known of the love Christ has for him.

Meet Juanita

Juanita is singing a chorus at youth choir rehearsal that is adapted from a verse in the book of James. The words, "Count it all joy" from James 1:2 make her happy to be a believer. Although she is popular and, by all indications, a normal teenager, Juanita is secretly preoccupied with the troubles of the world. She sees the world as sinking into oblivion and is not convinced that her future is assured to be successful. She prays about the injustices she sees and she trusts that God is also concerned. But she still feels a tinge of fear. The older she gets, the more aware she is that few things are certain in this world. Yet, the chorus she is singing reminds her that God will be there for her as her life unfolds.

Today's Teenagers

Making a list of the characteristics of today's young people would be the ultimate exercise in futility. They are very eclectic, choosing a bit from here and a little from there, so that words do not accurately describe this generation. In that reality comes our first attempt at offering some understanding of the youth in our churches.

While no two teenagers are exactly alike, some trends and characteristics surface as we consider today's young people. In the chapters following, we will examine these in detail.

As already mentioned, they are an eclectic group. Of great concern to them is the development of an "individualistic persona," one like no one else's. It is amazing that kids copy and wear styles that are very much like everyone else's, but with a belief that their particular style is completely different from all others. They put together dress packages which borrow from many different sources, including their parents, to become their own person. One national youth speaker suggests this is why parents wear such ugly clothes—to insure that their kids won't continually take their clothing!

Most western-world teens today know computers better than many adults. They seem to have a built-in ability to figure out technology. They have great awareness of the world. Buy a new electronic watch, video camera, or VCR and see who can operate it quickest—parent or teenager? In our house, our kids reset the watches and show us around the computer.

Clayton
70 kids
in ACE
4 left

With all of this sophistication and knowledge, however, teenagers today seem to be almost bankrupt in terms of maturity. Good church kids cause problems at school and in the home. In some major cities, adult involvement in criminal activity is actually on the decline but youth crimes are elevating at such a rapid rate the overall crime rates are ascending. Teenagers are involved in drug trafficking, murder, robbery, and all the rest.

Less than 20 years ago, in the late '70s and early '80s, the statistical data reflected about a 30% less involvement among church families in the juvenile justice system than of those in non-churched families. Today the numbers are almost identical.

Teenagers today are extremely tolerant and find it difficult to make a decision. They exhibit low motivation and are generally poorly committed to church, school, and family responsibilities. Too often their faith is linked to a relationship with other teenagers and not a loyalty to Christ.

This generation will take longer to graduate from college. Larger numbers will enroll later and many will drop out. Today's average teenager will shift her or his career from five to seven times before retirement. Without help, these kids will divorce in record numbers as married adults. As a generation, they will experience the frustration of earning less money than their parents. And they know this all too well.

It is no wonder that this generation so often expresses a hopelessness and answers many questions with, "I don't know." The fact is—they don't know.

It is troubling to note that from the time you read this page to 24 hours from now, some startling things will occur:

• Most teenagers will watch over three hours of TV and do only one hour of homework.

• Over 2,200 kids will decide to drop out of high school.

• 3,610 teenagers will be assaulted; 630 will be robbed, and about 80 will be raped.

• 500 teenagers will begin using illegal drugs and over 1,000 will try their first drink of alcohol.

• More than 100,000 students will carry a gun into their high school.

• 1,000 high school girls will become mothers outside of marriage.

Our world was never like theirs. And their world is not likely to go back to how it was for us.

Their Struggles

If we are going to help and guide these teens who need us, we need to recognize some of their struggles as *they* see them.

Teenagers raised in today's world are **extremely busy**. They have jobs just as we did. However, many have added to their jobs innumerable activities, lessons, school functions, church activities, and more. We had sports practices and other activities, too. But few of us had exposure to the scale of activity choices available to youth today.

Want to pacify a teenager? Turn on a video screen and feed their **strong video link**. The hypnotic effect of a screen upon most youth is almost amazing. This link is so intense that many schools are trying to make the most of it by teaching through monitors or computers instead of by real teachers. In college, these teenagers will have entire classes taught only through video.

Many teenagers do not know what to believe about faith and religion. They are confronted by a **myriad of religious choices** encompassing world religions, cults, the occult, and the various expressions of faith. Little guidance is offered by their peers, school, or society in sorting these choices out. Our kids want to know the differences, yet, society frowns upon an honest, critical comparison making the kids flounder even more.

Teenagers **feel that education is irrelevant** to life. Learning, to some degree, is geared to passing State mandated proficiency exams. Missing is the feeling and the drama behind the actual events or issues being taught. Facts learned are sometimes seen as useless and unconnected to real life.

For example, Mark recently visited the Auschwitz Concentration Camp near Krakow,

Poland. Upon his return to the United States, he shared some of his feelings with the youth at church. The overwhelming response was, "Why haven't we been taught any of this?" Most of the high schoolers knew nothing of this horrendous blemish upon human history.

Kids today seem to **dichotomize life between the secular and the sacred**. It is becoming more and more natural for them to have a church life and a very different life the rest of the week. Mark has worked with church kids who genuinely loved Christ and yet were mixed up in selling illegal substances. In working with them, he was shocked to hear them relate how their spiritual life was separate from their secular life. Somehow they managed to separate the two without feeling a conflict. And, obviously, they had not found a moral compass to truth in the Bible.

With this is the **resurgence of drug and alcohol use** among youth. Again, there is little statistical differentiation between churched and non-churched kids. From smoking cigarettes to the use of addictive narcotics, the evidence is that our nation's drug education is not working. Many remain in the "Just Say No" mentality until they reach high school where close to 80% of all kids will experiment with a substance that alters their perceptions.

Having **too many opportunities and choices** is a stressful challenge for kids. They have far more entertainment, scholastic, athletic, and leisure alternatives available to compete for their time and energies. As a result, a significant number will make no choices. They feel short circuited as they weigh the advantages and disadvantages of each opportunity and try to experience all or as much of life as possible as quickly as possible. They are afraid of missing out on something.

Some kids, though, stay home because they cannot decide between church camp, work camp, the canoe adventure, or the bike trip. The choices create **a sensory and decision-making overload** making it easier to do nothing than choose one and maybe miss out on something that was better.

Coupled with this issue, teenagers find **difficulty in making appropriate choices.** With so many options, so many opportunities, so many ways to go, how can they know which choices to make? It is disturbing to be confronted with nearly 100 class choices when making out a class schedule. Kids have asked Mark why they can't just learn the basics of a solid education.

Life can be upsetting when the structure of **the family is in flux.** In our youth we faced a much different set of socially accepted conditions. Twenty-five years ago, Mark was the only kid in his senior high youth group with divorced parents who participated actively. In some youth groups, almost half of the kids come from broken homes. Add to this the new family model of both parents working full time and families moving frequently. Too many kids have learned to feel that nothing lasts. Why get attached?

Other issues include their tendency toward **poor commitment** to anything; the position of

high tolerance even when they may disagree with an issue; the fact that many exhibit **low motivation** in most areas of life and hold great **doubt about the future.** Not the most positive of pictures, yet each of these factors must be acknowledged in the life of your youth ministry. It is in the midst of all of this that the message of salvation through Jesus Christ alone and full-time commitment to Him is to be communicated to this generation.

Welcome to the Adventure

Enough of the bleaker aspects of today's youth culture. Even such a brief overview can make us want to hide our heads. However, Christ has called and commissioned us to reach out beyond the circumstances and share the Good News. The task is difficult, but it is not impossible. It is an adventure of faith.

We must not lose sight of the obstacles and barriers which our ministries will encounter in our work with young people. But we must never lose heart. The rapid pace of change in today's world cannot be allowed to overshadow the truth of God's gift of salvation in Jesus Christ. The assurance that there is an eternal, changeless absolute of faith and truth meets the deepest cry of every heart. We have a challenge, but we also have the hand of God directing our teaching ministry in the Sunday School, the Christian high school, the youth club, and the youth group.

This book is designed to encourage your involvement on this adventure. There are important considerations in developing a successful teaching ministry to your church's teenagers. This book will look at many of them.

The truths of God's Word hold a world of wonder for today's high school teenager. Their world is exciting, yet changing swiftly; we dare not find ourselves short in making the message of Christ relevant.

Mark found himself in church from day one. He knew the stories and the basic teachings of the Bible, but could find no bridge between what his teachers were sharing and his life. Then a church member, Jo, took the high school class and changed all of that. Her secret? She listened to us, learned about our struggles, and then showed how the truths of the Bible related to our world. It literally set into motion the changes in his heart needed to see how God's ways could daily become a part of his life. It was a revolutionary discovery. Jo made the Bible and Christianity come alive for all of us.

And you will, too. God has placed you before the teenagers in your church to make a difference, planting seeds of truth and faith into hearts too long dominated by the forces at work in this world. Don't cling to the 1950s styles of teaching in a room of teens anticipating a new millennium. Welcome new ideas as innovative tools that will enable you to communicate more clearly to kids often deafened by the roaring winds of change!

2 Who Are Today's High Schoolers?

One of Mark's favorite high school youth group meetings occurs during the first gathering of every New Year. He rounds up the kids and leads them through the composing of a letter which they write to themselves.

After distributing plenty of pens and paper and an envelope, he encourages them to write as detailed an account of their lives today as they possibly can. This is all we do for the entire 90 minute meeting. He lists the following thoughts or questions.

- How is life for you these days?
- What is going on at home, at school, at church?
- What are the big news stories for you?
- What is troubling you about your life, your family, your world?
- How is your relationship with God?
- What are you learning about Him?
- What are your major personal concerns?
- What problems are you facing?
- List some goals for the next 365 days.
- What are your favorite songs, favorite classes?
- Who are your good buddies?
- Guess what might change in your life this year.
- What are your hopes and dreams for this year? for the next five years?

And finally,

• Write a special, personal prayer to God for your New Year.

After the letters are written, each teenager inserts their letter into an envelop and addresses it to themselves, sealing it. Mark collects them and saves them for a year, mailing them back about two weeks before the current year ends.

The response over the 12 years that he has done this has been incredible. The most common reaction—"I can't believe how much I have changed! Look at how I've grown!"

Youth ministry can be a gauge by which each teenager in the church discovers who they are before God and as a person in whom God the Holy Spirit resides. That is why we, as teachers and leaders, are not simply helpers or guides. We are ministers and servants. We are authorized representatives of the God of the universe. We are Ambassadors for Jesus Christ.

Under our leadership, high school youth will travel through significant developmental stages of their lives. A ninth or tenth grader is very different from a graduating senior. Yet, not so long ago, each senior was an underclass student just starting out in high school. We often marvel at the annual ritual in which juniors and seniors ask us if they were ever as goofy, immature, and clueless as the current batch of younger kids. They ask, "Did we act like that? Were we ever that weird?" Of course, they were. But you helped shape their advances to maturity.

Young people experience a wide range of physical, emotional, mental, social, and moral changes as they grow toward adulthood. Each of these changes is influenced by what is, perhaps, our most important foundational concern as church leaders—the spiritual growth of each student. A solid spiritual foundation will temper the potential storms of each of the other developmental area.

It must be noted that no two teenagers are alike in every way. While we know this in our hearts, we often forget it in our heads as we teach. We need to constantly remind ourselves that high schoolers are not "peas in a pod."

As we look at an overview of the developmental stages and tasks mentioned above, please remember that this is only an overview. It is useful to understand trends and the basic developmental challenges that teenagers face. However, it is not an exhaustive accounting, nor does it examine the areas of difficulty which may plague some of the youth in your class. For a look at some of the more difficult youth ministry challenges, get a copy of *Ministering To Kids Who Don't Fit* (Accent Publications, Mark Simone). Interestingly, although it is a youth leadership manual, many parents of challenging teenagers are using it as a parenting aid.

Your role is leader, guide, friend, and partner with the parents of these teens. Your influence may, for awhile, become greater than their parents'. Understand them from the inside out.

Let's look at some specific information about teenage developmental issues.

An Overall Word

For most of our churches, the age and grade range of our high school classes and youth programs will encompass four grades, 9 through 12, and roughly the ages between 15 and 18. On its own, this is a tremendous challenge filled with diversity.

However, add to this the simple fact that development at every level is not so polite as to be on any time table. The kids develop physically as their bodies determine. Social development is linked to social experiences. Mental and emotional developments have their own criteria. And so on.

In approaching your class, keep in mind that the life and experiences of a normal, Christian high school freshman are worlds apart from those of a graduating senior. Stir in a liberal dose of life experiences like divorce, multiple moves, illness, or even being shy, and the matter gets even more complex. One cannot over-invest in information about normal teenage development. In fact, assume that they are all completely different and be pleasantly surprised when two kids actually do want to discuss the same thing!

While spiritual commitment and growth is vital, sometimes we neglect other areas of basic, normal development. However, God designed each developmental area to work in *harmony* and *balance* with the other areas. If one area is accentuated in importance and the others are treated as "less spiritual," then the outcome is to isolate our Christianity from everyday life. The dangerous assumption is that if we primarily concentrate on the spiritual, the other areas will somehow fall into place. This, however, does not "naturally" happen.

Genesis 1 tells us God looked on His creation as being good. This endorsement included humans. Paul, in Ephesians 4:16, reminds us that Christ makes the whole body join together for an "effectual working." This integration insures our ability to serve God and work with others.

God designed the developmental processes we experience. It is part of the plan of God, allowing us to "grow up into him in all things" (Ephesians 4:15). Even Jesus "increased in wisdom and stature" (Luke 2:52).

It is a holy thing and very important that these developmental stages be respected and observed in the lives of our teenagers. As you work through the following areas, reflect on your own experiences in these stages and look to see how God used them to make you who you are today. Jesus, fully God yet fully human, also moved through these developmental stages. Such thoughts help us find grace for the raging hormones and silly behavior our teenage students often display.

Physical Development

The high school years are often called the years of drastic sexual maturation and dramatic physical growth. However, it seems that these features describe much of the teenager's years if left only to the perceptions of the popular media. Those who work with teenagers know that this is only a small part of the package. Yet, it is an important part.

In these years young women develop the ability to reproduce and carry life. Their hormones change; natural deposits of tissue and fat change their body shape. Some experience a change in voice. On all fronts they get "new" bodies. And the boys begin to notice.

The young men experience similar changes in height, body, and voice. In addition, they sprout facial and body hair and find that their muscles can now be shaped and developed. Teenaged boys fight with clumsiness in this stage when even walking is a chore. Most boys will be dissatisfied with the height they attain or their level of strength. The girls are beginning to notice them, as well.

There are plenty of excellent books which focus entirely on these physical developments. The point is that their bodies are in massive flux, and they often feel like strangers to themselves. These changes can cause tremendous worries which come with a growing body. Teenagers fear developing too early or too late. They worry about being different. Virtually all girls will be dissatisfied with the changes in their bodies. Boys often try to ignore the maturation process and deny their need for a shower and some deodorant. It is in these changing bodies they attend your class or youth activities.

Let's consider how these physical changes will impact your classroom.

These physical developments lend themselves to "pecking orders" which often are not based upon who makes the best leaders in the group. Big boys get lots of regard and are frequently deferred to as leaders, even if only unofficially. Girls with the best hair, prettiest face, or most feminine body may be deferred to or seen as the most suitable for regard. Unfortunately, this leaves lots of kids in the dust and may not bode well for your program if the "Beautiful People" actually do call all of the shots in planning and participation.

Underdeveloped kids often try to hide by being quiet or unassuming. They need our help in equaling the playing field by drawing them into the program. Treat each teenager as equally as possible. Be aware that you are also susceptible to the influence of society and the media. Be alert. You, too, may be drawn to respecting the teenagers who seem to look more adult, to be the "jocks," or the "cheerleaders." This is not a fair system of reference.

Do not classify a teenager by her or his physical development or lack of development. The body is only a vessel; the inner person is who we teach. In other words, don't judge the book by its cover. Remember I Samuel 16:7? Man looks at the outward appearance. But it's who is inside that God sees. Help them understand the physical changes, but do not use them as a means through which you assume their maturity or worth.

Here are some important points of physical development to keep in mind:

• Girls tend to mature well before boys.
• Physical development often causes much trauma.

• If they develop too fast or too slow, they are embarrassed and sensitive about it.

• Most teenagers are not happy about obvious development.

• They lack useful, accurate developmental information and live on rumor and assumptions.

• Undisciplined hormones may lead them into trouble.

• A changing body is a body they feel they cannot trust.

God, through the human life of Jesus, reached out to us as "body persons." God wants us to love, respect, and care for our bodies in all of their developmental stages. Teach kids to be comfortable with these changes by helping them feel comfortable with what's coming. Incorporate good information in your program as you teach them to develop their faith. This is a gift for which they will long remember you.

Emotional Development

The flood of hormonal changes in young men and women is accompanied by fluctuations of the emotions. These ups and downs can be significant. Expect eruptions of anger and uncontrollable laughter. Look for the kids who usually have good attitudes to become moody, depressed, or grouchy. Some kids will metamorphose into completely different teenagers. All-in-all, emotional development should be seen as a roller coaster.

The emotional development of the teenagers in your classroom will begin to include deeper levels of common feelings like joy, love, fear, etc. Defined as "an intense mental state arising subjectively rather than mentally or consciously," it is easy to see how emotions can be experienced in such ranges. Feelings are not governed by what we think or how we reason and often seem to simply "come over us." Yet, God gave them to us so they must be pretty marvelous.

Keep in mind the following key points about teenage emotional development.

• Teenagers experience emotions in many differing ways.

• Emotions are troubling to most teens because they are so uncontrollable.

• Most teenagers do not understand their emotions.

• Emotional maturity needs nurture to insure healthy development.

• A crisis can arrest emotional growth, keeping the teenager emotional underdeveloped.

• Emotional growth and development has been largely overlooked by psychologists and is being researched for the significant role it plays in our lives.

The emotional health of a teenager is fostered through careful attention to the appropriateness of responses to situations. In the classroom this may take on the face of an impassioned outburst in the middle of a topic which, on the surface, makes no sense.

Recently we were discussing relationships, love, and what makes a Christian marriage. At an especially non-controversial moment, one young man made some belittling comments about marriage, God, and the uselessness of women. The room exploded in argument and debate with most of the kids disagreeing with the fellow. I, however, knew that the source of his comments were founded in the news that his parents were going to divorce. Marriage was no longer a secure, holy thing to him.

Juveniles trip over their emotions more than any other developmental area. Many times, the things said, the reactions, the outbursts, the off-color and inappropriate comments all add up to surprise them. They are as shocked as we may be.

Love them into appropriate, mature emotional reactions and help them understand that control is sometimes difficult. Let them see they are normal in their emotional clumsiness. And assure them that Jesus' love and forgiveness are constant, even when our emotions misfire.

Mental Development

Some convincingly argue that this is one developmental area teenagers seem to consistently avoid. Yet, God is working!

Kids today face major obstacles in their mental development on a number of fronts. First, they have access to great amounts of information and huge technical advances. They have the data, but lack the application how-to. Knowing too much is sometimes a liability when common sense and experience are not in place to temper the facts acquired. The focus seems to be on what the high school student knows with little regard for the practical application. Unfortunately, this is why there are so many unwed teen pregnancies each year.

Secondly, learning facts is no assurance that the teenager is learning how to think. It is better to teach a kid the skills of thoughtful deliberation instead of rote learning of material. Material can be accessed quite easily, but determining how to use the factual material is an altogether different animal.

Thirdly, there is too much pressure on "blind acceptance" among our teenagers. Questioning and analyzing skills are overlooked. Blindly accepting a value, often a peer pressure, without questioning the end results or morality of the action leads to irresponsibility. Teenagers need to feel comfortable in asking questions and analyzing the answers.

To be a Christian is not to forego careful examination. We conduct "Bible *Study*," not "Brainless Bible Reception." Paul encouraged Timothy to, "study to shew thyself approved unto God..." (II Timothy 2:15) The Greek word used for "study" means to make effort, labor and endeavor, and give diligence in our study of God's Word.

As you teach your high schoolers, keep in mind:

• Learning styles will differ among the students.

• They may need permission to ponder the truth in the message.

• Mental development takes time.

• There are gaps between concrete thinking and abstract thinking which may require explanation.

• Mental development cannot be gauged or assessed by a test, recitation of facts, or debate.

Finally, there are areas where faith has to supersede knowledge. The Bible teaches that knowledge makes us big-headed (I Corinthians 8:1), but love makes the difference. We have never seen God physically, but we believe. Science and secular society may scream "No way! God cannot exist if I cannot see Him!" But our teens need to know that they can trust their relationship with God, the testimony of the saints, and the inner assurance of the Holy Spirit. Faith believes that the air we breath gives us life, even if we can't see it.

Social Development

Oh, the joys of watching teenagers stumble and bumble through all the things they learn in their social developments. Furtive glances from the guys to the girls. Too loud conversations meant to be heard by everyone but pretending to be secret. Monosyllabic answers to intimate or heady questions. Preening and promenading. And what about those outfits?

Our ministries have the opportunity of being a great source of help to teenagers facing the challenges and tasks of developing socially. For some it seems to be almost inborn. For most, the interactions are a sort of "laboratory" from which they experiment in hopes of finding answers.

28

Through our leadership, we can teach appropriate social skills to teenagers truly afraid of doing the wrong thing.

Once Mark led an entire youth group through an understanding of which fork is used for what, putting the napkin on the lap, and not talking with mouths full while eating in a nice restaurant because a few of the kids did not know what to do. No one felt "dumb," because he treated it lightheartedly and taught everyone. This may not sound "spiritual, " but the activity showed the kids he cared, and they trusted him more.

When kids don't quite know what to do, how to act, or what to say, they feel very uncomfortable. In our work we have held make-up parties, discussed hygiene, shared which type of clothing is best suited for which occasions, and other socially important behaviors. In doing so, we have reduced the immense social pressures our developing young adults feel. When dating is figured into the equation, these skills reduced potentially embarrassing situations.

The weight teens place on social behavior is formidable. Teenagers have no frame of reference through which they can determine what is appropriate or inappropriate. It is all new to them. From the first date, to conversation, to etiquette, to how a Christian acts when spending time with the opposite sex, it is all important information. It's still ministry.

Some things to keep in mind:
• It is OK to assume they do not know.

- Be gentle in correction to avoid embarrassing them.
- They often need to be reminded.
- Discipline is appropriate if they create social disturbances.
- Most will appreciate your concern.
- You were there once.

So often our witness for Christ is measured by our behavior. Teaching kids how to behave in social settings, while remembering they are still adolescents, is a wonderful gift to offer. Have a girls only retreat and talk about make-up, hair, dating, and the hormonal make-up of boys. Have a guys retreat and talk about hygiene, how to treat a girl, body building, and hot rods. And do each of them from both perspectives. Have a husband/ wife team present at both retreats. Your encouragement will enable them to advance through one of the most frustrating aspects of growing up they face. And, social instruction can help them avoid temptation through ignorance.

Moral Development

We live in a time when the TV is used to raise kids. Personally, we find very little worth trusting for our own kids. This is why we had cable television removed from our home.

Morals are not simply absorbed by virtue of being around nice folks. Nor are they inbred when Christians have children. In fact, the Hebrews understood this so well that they devoted training time to moral instruction. Today, we call the record of this training the book of Proverbs.

Our culture is markedly immoral, and not just from the Christian perspective. Murder, robbery, drugs, rape, abuse, and sexual misconduct have become the fodder for most news reporting, printed entertainment, and TV situations. Music portrays sexual opportunities explicitly, rather than the old teenagers falling in love motif most of us grew up listening to. Families in sitcoms are ridiculed; parents are morons. The rich and beautiful are the icons of our imitation. Violence permeates almost every issue of life on TV dramas. Homosexuality is an acceptable alternative lifestyle. Those who have religious faith are portrayed as psychopathic, ineffectual, or just ignored and left out of all consideration.

Unfortunately, Christian teenagers are not raised in a protective vacuum. They deal in the world daily and are influenced by what they see. We have visited kids from our church in jails or detention centers who acted out and were caught. The shock is when some of those kids seem surprised that their crimes or misbehaviors caused so much fervor.

Add to this the fact that TV programs produce workable solutions to any problem in 30 or 60 minutes, and you have quite a confusing condition.

None of this moral turmoil is lost on our high schoolers.

Teens see families in conflict. They see adults divorcing, abusing, lying, doing wrong, not caring about church, and not pleasing God. To many, the moral discrepancies are why they quit going to church after graduation.

Moral development must begin in the home at an early age. But for the high school youth leader, it must be reinforced on all fronts—study, discussion, example, training. Scripture carefully taught can teach morality missing from the home. Those who did learn moral truth as an outgrowth of mature faith at home need the fortification of relevant application within the peer group they face as high schoolers. Most teens believe in absolutes of right and wrong. You can give them the biblical standard they long for.

Of moral development, remember:

• What is seen is more impressive than what is said.

• Many potential moral models like teachers, coaches, even pastors, have fallen short with their own problems.

• Teenagers need constant help in being morally vigilant.

• Society will undermine your efforts and teach them that many problematic behaviors are normal.

God's standards of human interaction and behavior are challenged in the teen years by hormones and the independence most teenagers crave. As leaders we have a responsibility and a privilege to stand as the example they need to persevere.

Spiritual Development

We look at this area last because we want it fresh in your minds. This is the one area which will endure, undergird, and direct the young adult in each of the other areas throughout their lives. Although each area develops throughout life, only the spiritual reaps eternal dividends. When teenagers accept a committed Christian life as their life, their sensitivity to the guidance and direction of the Holy Spirit will ease them through the hardships and changes of the others.

God's claim on lives begins in the womb, as David expressed in Psalm 22:9-10 and Psalm 139:13. From conception to death, we grow in a better understanding of God's love for us. As children this development begins by learning the stories of the Bible and being assured of God's unconditional love.

As teenagers, this love meets challenge. It is common for high school students to challenge the faith of their parents and their church. This is a normal part of life and results in owning one's faith personally, deeply, from conviction, not as an extension of the parents' or the church's dictum. We must all accept Jesus on our own, and we must each accept His Lordship as our reasonable service (Romans 12:1-2).

Teenagers are often very interested in other expressions of faith. They often expand beyond our comfort levels in seeking "other gods." It is part of their expanding understanding of the world and their hesitation to exclude others of different religious positions. Your job is to hear their questions and to reaffirm the sole basis of genuine Christianity—faith in Jesus Christ alone (I John 2).

We cannot slander other religions, nor demean their ceremonies for this is a sure way to turn a teenager into a blind supporter of what is perceived as the "underdog." However, most teens are open to honest truth about other religions if we will spend some time talking about them and affirming why we are followers of Jesus. Our openness is consistent with their need for fairness. Doing this strengthens their relationship with Christ and with us. Helping them "check it out" takes away a potential power struggle and gives our teens room to grow in their faith.

Studies show that young people are very interested in spiritual issues. They also show that we, as adults, parents, and leaders, blunder when we present our faith as the only position without adequate explanation. Often teens will question our stances and suspiciously wonder about our conclusions, so it is more effective to allow them room to question, see the differences, know what God's Word says, and arrive at a personal conclusion based on faith and God's Word. Be open to questions and prepared to explain how to use the Bible as the sole litmus test against which all other beliefs must be held.

These normal questions about other religions makes your youth group an excellent place to look at the various positions and beliefs.

Teenagers are intrigued by the various doctrinal differences when compared under equal headings. For example, baptism, communion, fellowship, and distinct doctrinal positions can be discussed in terms of the differences held by various denominations. High schoolers find it most interesting to study differences. Use this God-given curiosity to anchor them in their faith, their confidence in God's Word, and their dependence upon Jesus Christ alone.

We are not working with dry paint or set concrete when we teach teenagers. Each one is a miracle, and each is different from the rest. Yet, in general, they flow through the same waters in terms of who they are becoming. Their struggles, challenges, fears, and successes are much the same. As you help them negotiate the tough times and uncertain waters in the name of Jesus, you show them a loving Christ who cares for them. What a great gift to pass on!

3 *Leaders and Growth*

A number of distractions keep young adults away from the spiritual information or experiences they need for hearty growth. We believe in the necessity of a "firm foundation," building upon the example and work of Christ. Yet, an enemy would place obstacles in our way to keep us from serving God. Therefore, the first thing we need is an awareness of the things that keep *us* from teaching high schoolers. Some of these are in us; some are in the kids or their culture.

■ *Blind Spots.* Every program and every leader has some significant blind spots. A blind spot is something that prevents us from clearly seeing what it is we need to be doing. It may be a personal quirk, a community custom, or some scheduling problem in the church. Maybe it's a long-standing special service that conflicts with a significant youth ministry opportunity. When some distracting aspect continually keeps you from effective ministry, you're being nailed by a blind spot.

For example, a youth minister colleague noted that his mid-week teen program was continually butting head with the high school sports schedule. For years he tried to do battle, losing continually to the school practice timetable. Frustrated, he finally sought help from the parents of his youth group members. One mom suggested they move youth group back an hour and offer a meal, served and prepared by the parents. The competition was eliminated by removing a blind spot.

■ *The Long Run.* Too often we plan for the short run and overlook our small incremental influence over time. The Long Run is so important to youth ministry. It is the factor most often missing in consistent, mature growth. It can only come from and through us, as the adult leaders and teachers.

Kids need us to give them the time it takes to hear, consider, question, adapt, and appropriate the things of God for their personal lives. This is not done in a few lessons, or in one semester of Sunday School classes. Learning is a very personal *process* with each student learning differently. Therefore, it is important to plot a course over time that builds upon what has already been learned.

What's needed

Our youth need many things from us which, by and large, we feel honored offering. These are the materials from which lifelong relationships are built. For many of us, there are some specific gifts we give the kids when we teach.

Continuity. We have all seen the disasters left behind when a youth pastor or youth leader leaves the youth group for a new church, using the group being left as a steppingstone to a better offer. It takes quite a while, under normal circumstances, for a group of young adults to accept and trust a leader. If a leader stays only a few months, or even a year, then the time it takes to open up to and trust the next leader is increased. It takes a commitment from the youth leader to the kids and to the church for effective ministry to develop.

This is as true for volunteer leadership or teachers as it is for paid youth pastors. Each person undertaking a teaching post needs to take the commitment very seriously. The kids certainly do. It is also important to realize that if we walk away from our obligation prematurely, we cause some damage to the teens and make it very difficult for the next teacher.

Continuity is a gift of the certainty of your presence that the kids find essential. They look to you for your leadership, but they also need your adult friendship and commitment to them. To treat the position of teacher as trivial or transient is wrong. Whether they openly acknowledge or not, you become an important factor in how they perceive faith and daily living. It does no good to recite the words of Jesus that "I will never leave or forsake you" and then decide that teaching or this church is not for you.

Of course, sometimes life, health, family, work, or other dynamics require us to break our commitment. We resign. But even this can become a teaching-learning opportunity.

Openly communicate the reasons you must leave the class, but avoid any complaints or gossip, especially involving the church or its leadership. Share only what is good and appropriate, remembering that the kids will remain in the care of the church, and you are still building their respect for the church.

Teach that life is unpredictable and we must always remain open to new areas into which God leads us. Allow the kids time to grieve. Be aware that they may react with anger, confusion, and hurt—but let them express it and address it.

Your best work, if you leave, will be to plant the seeds that will enable the new youth leader to pick up and continue the good work which you have begun.

Room to grow. A wonderful junior high aged young man we'll call Jimmy was an original member in Mark's first youth group. He had a natural style of evangelism, reaching out to his friends and peers to invite them to youth group. Single-handedly, Jimmy nearly doubled the amount of kids Mark began with.

Mark soon came to know Jimmy for his pranks, his smart mouth, and his larger than life stories. Unfortunately, Mark forgot to allow for normal and natural maturity and growth. When Jimmy grew up and began acting like a young adult in his high school years, Mark continued to treat Jimmy as the junior high kid he'd met early on and loved as he was becoming a man. To say the least, Jimmy did not appreciate it when Mark treated him as a child in front of his high school peers. Finally, Jimmy taught Mark a wonderful lesson by gently reminding him that he was no longer a child.

In our work with high schoolers, many of us will know the kids from their very early days. We delight in watching them grow up, but we must remember that they are no longer the children we once knew. They need us to allow them room to mature and the freedom to change into the people God intends them to become.

Honesty. Why is it sometimes so hard to admit to the kids that we just do not know? Why can't we say that freely and model to them that answers are sought and learned throughout life? Not to stereotype, but this seems to be more of a problem with men than women. Secular society says men are weak if they don't know everything. We sometimes let this mindset carry over into ministry.

It can be liberating and a great example to say, "I don't know" with the promise that you'll find out by next week. It teaches the high school student that the Christian life is gathered in bits and pieces of knowledge and spurts of growth along the path that God calls us to follow. We learn and mature from day to day.

Another aspect of honesty is to be who we are and not who we think the kids want us to be. Being who God made us as we help them find who God created them to be is effective discipleship training.

One of the single most important examples of honesty which will affect your kids long after they've left your youth group is the ability to say, "I'm sorry." Or, "I was wrong; please forgive me."

It only creates more harm if you refuse to be humble and honest when you do make mistakes. No one is perfect. The kids won't believe you for long about anything if you try to bluff through mistakes.

Your life and your attitudes toward humility, servanthood, compassion, prejudices, truth will teach lessons your words alone never can. The Lord hates seven things: "...a proud look, a lying tongue, and hands that shed innocent blood. An heart that deviseth wicked imaginations, feet that be swift in running to mischief, a false witness that speaketh lies, and he that soweth discord among brethren" (Proverbs 6:16-19). Is your life honest before the Lord and before the kids?

Honesty is the foundation for every effective youth ministry. It is the bedrock for trust in what you teach as well as the example you live.

Guidance by example. The kids need for us to lead the way through our lives, not our words. This crucial need gives high schoolers encouragement and hope as they see you press through your challenges into the solutions.

In the past our family has had to trust God and live through many troubling health difficulties. For the most part we have been open about our illnesses, asking the teenagers to pray for us and keeping them posted on what we learn from the doctors or which procedures we may face. God has been faithful, and the kids in our youth groups have learned that God will be there with us in the darkest times, providing light and hope.

We have been honest and open in our doubts and when we received less that glowing reports. With such guidance by example we have provided the teenagers with an opportunity to learn in ways not covered in a curriculum or study guides.

Linking such life examples to lessons is an effective way to help them cross the bridge between information and application. They need us to be witnesses as to how our faith is tested in daily living with all of the challenges and trials.

Fellowship. Christian kids need to be with Christian kids. They need a place that is safe, open, and lends itself to sharing with others of similar beliefs.

In our communities we have few places where Christian kids can be comfortable in who they are in Christ. In "public" they may be ridiculed and embarrassed for believing in the Bible or following Jesus. Let's face it, it is hard for most of us as adults to stand against the teasing or laughter of those outside of the faith. Why do we expect it to be less challenging for our youth, who are unseasoned and often confused or divided between wanting to please their friends and God? If we can provide a place in our youth group which encourages fellowship, we meet a significant need.

Currently, in our church, we are hearing from the kids what a haven youth group has become. Our community is being plagued by drug and alcohol abuse. Many parents in the community seem to feel that it will "go away" in time. Others have determined that this is simply the way things are. Yet, we hear over and over again from the kids that they appreciate a place to come, even for a few hours, where they can be with others who are trying to resist.

When teenagers are given the opportunity to be together in dialogue about social or teenage problems, they learn that their peers also face these hazards. They discover they are not alone in the fight. Strength develops in the numbers and friendships which are made. Together, they find solutions.

These are but a few of the kinds of needs that our children have. As a youth group leader and/or Sunday School teacher, you can find yourself only planning for the things you think they want and overlooking the social and spiritual needs they face.

Granted, most young people are unaware of these kinds of needs. They want lives that are fun, exciting, and entertaining. Today's youth seek the moment with little realization of the ramifications or consequences. Planning in some of these needs with a healthy dose of their wants makes in far more likely that they will support the program. It also does wonders for insuring they will participate.

We are not proposing a "Needs *versus* Wants" decision-making model. Rather, we find that in planning for the *Long Run* with an awareness of the occasional *Blind Spots* makes for good balance within a meaningful and relevant program. Work with and through the pastor and Sunday School superintendent in your church. That person will likely support you in your fine tuning. Don't be a renegade!

Psychologists tell us that today's teenagers are the most diverse group of teenagers ever produced in the history of our planet. With so many sources of information, and not all of them good, they truly are confused and uncertain. Become an expert on the kids in your class and pray for the sensitivity to help them with their needs.

Recently, we had two active high schoolers deeply grieving over the death of their grandfathers. Of course, their friends shared their pain. We had prayed about these two grandpas, asking God to touch them and be present in their lives and bodies. Both of the men died within a week of the other.

Such developments change the needs of the group and require our delicate attention in making Christ and His love real in the lives affected. Showing that God did not fail, that He was faithful to the two men and their grandchildren, that His love led these godly men into their life with Him were all comforting words which met needs. The rest of the group, while being supportive to the two in grief, were also being prepared for the inevitable deaths of their own grandparents. This is ministering to the needs of our classes.

Consider the other kinds of needs which our youth face. Aside from drugs and alcohol problems or the death of loved ones, they also must come to grips with such dissimilar issues as their budding sexuality, respect of adults and authority, friendship, dating relationships, secular relationships, their Christian witness, a growing understanding of God, career or college preparation, illness, and all the rest. As teachers we must recognize that these are also spiritual needs, never forgetting that we, in our youth, also had to learn how a Christian works through such problems or challenges. Helping them face these in the classroom is an excellent "jump start" to the more complex tasks of adulthood.

In Christ, our needs are either met or tempered according to His will. In our classrooms these valuable and essential issues can be discussed, modeled, studied, and prayed for with appropriate love and concern. Far better that we, as spiritual leaders, guide these discussions than to leave them to the perspectives of uninformed friends, non-Christians, or the media.

If we allow our classes to become holy laboratories where every issue is allowed, every question considered, every want and need examined, we will make a difference for Christ in the lives of these incredible students He has given us. We will become positive agents of growth—in their lives and in our own.

4 Our Needs As Teachers

Let's get honest and admit that we, as leaders and teachers, have needs, too. It is okay to declare that we relish sharing with the youth of our churches. We enjoy them, for the most part, and feel blessed to be investing in their spiritual growth. However, it is a lot more than just a "feel good" investment. It is also part of our own spiritual development and "reasonable service" to Christ. For many of us, to not teach is as unimaginable as blueless skies or grass that is orange. It is our calling from God. This is our "flock," our place of ministry.

Just the ability to teach does not equip us to be the right youth leader for the teenagers in our church, though. Like anything of worth or value, it takes preparation and a continual honing of our communication and teaching skills, as well as an ongoing understanding of today's youth and their culture. We must be students of our teenagers, of their interests, fears, worries, delights, and con-temporary heroes.

Our ministries must be an extension of our personal development in service to God. Being a natural communicator or a gifted teacher does not guarantee that we are effective in leading teenagers into a deeper relationship with Jesus. Faith is shared heart-to-heart. Kids can spot insincerity, phoniness, judgmentalism, and intolerance at the classroom door. These are the kinds of baggage which will reduce our ministry effectiveness to *nil* in no time.

This chapter looks at ourselves as leaders and teachers. It is not intended to call our gifts into question or to examine our motivation. Rather, it is a look at our belief that teachers are made, not born. Teaching is not a birthright. It is a gift of God. We become teachers as we invest in ourselves and in our study of God's Word.

Both of us have worked with many teachers in our nearly two decades as a youth minister or Christian education coordinator. The surprising factor is that the best teachers are not always the best prepared or the greatest speakers. Many times the most effective teacher is the one who can relate to their class personally, as well as understand their culture. Be it a teacher of children or toddlers, single adults or the elderly, young or older married, if the teacher can relate to the difficulties and challenges of the age group and relate the gospel to life in that slot, more often than not, they do very well.

Char was an interesting and devoted young woman who wanted to work with our junior high youth. The church invested some money in her training, sending her to training events and doing what we could to prepare her for this challenging age group. She had heart, spunk, and a commitment to her charges. But she could not adapt her style of leadership to encompass the needs of this age group. She was rigid and an intellectual; they needed someone patient and flexible. She flopped in teaching—until we moved her to leading the post-high school young adults group. Then she was a shining star.

Conversely, Allan was an older adult with only a high school diploma who worked on an assembly line. He was a bright and dear Christian, but his chances of taking on that class with any level of success seemed to be "slim and none." Yet, Allan became the junior high leader and Sunday School teacher for years with incredible success. His secret? He spent his preparation time "hanging with" the junior highers and learning their world. Then, he applied his growing knowledge of Scripture to the particular needs of the age group. He skillfully inserted Jesus into every question or void.

Neither Char nor Allen were "born teachers." They accepted these roles as part of their service to Christ. Each succeeded when their skills and gifts met the right need and could adapt their gifts to relate to their constituencies.

As you prepare to teach high school aged teenagers, ask and answer these questions.

• *Why do I want to work with high schoolers?*

What drives you to accept the responsibility to prepare a weekly lesson for these kids? Is it masochism, stupidity, or an inability to give up our own youth?

No. Usually, it is a need we have to help others. It feels good to be involved. It is also good to be part of something which is larger than ourselves when we show young people the way to eternal life and spiritual growth.

Perhaps you teach to pass on the heritage of our faith. Maybe it is to make some small, yet powerful, difference in this world through the changed lives of the youth you serve. Hopefully, it's not because your pastor cornered you to help out on a day when your guard was down!

Whatever the reason, the desire to teach these kids stirs your heart. However, in many ways the next question is the more important one:

• *What do I need from teaching high schoolers?*

This is an important question to answer or you may miss the joy in how the giver receives as much as he gives. When we introduce Christ and a life of serving Him with others, we find ourselves drawing closer to Him.

Needs and being needy are important in our faith. It helps us to become interdependent with the church in ways which are healthy and wholesome. To need is to accept the fact that we cannot go it alone. Paul's beautiful words on the body of Christ remind us that God expects us to all work together as one (I Corinthians 12).

Scripture promises that "...God will supply all your need" (Philippians 4:19). God creates us to be needy and then meets our needs. To not recognize that we are needy would be to position ourselves against God's sovereignty. Needing to receive is a good thing and helps us as "the sheep of His pasture," not the opposite.

Some of us need to be useful or appreciated. Others need to be looked up to as leaders. There are those among us who find it compelling to share the knowledge and experiences of the Christian life that they have accumulated. Others feel a spiritual obligation to work for the church.

The reasons vary from teacher to teacher. A fellow teacher may express reasons quite different from your own. Comparison is not the best indicator; your own heart is.

Accepting our need to teach, and realizing that through our need will come some of God's finest work in our lives, let's look at some of the areas which can limit the effectiveness of our work with high school teenagers.

Spotting Red Flags

We have to be aware of potential pitfalls in working with high school young adults or we will be "sunk" before we conclude our first session. Based on who they are at this age, we have to adapt our words and approaches to remain relevant to them. If we do not, they will refuse to hear us, believing that we are unable to understand them or their struggles.

When Mark was in high school, he loved singing in the school choir. In his first year, he was intimidated by a group of rather unruly upperclassmen who liked to toss barbs at the choir director.

One afternoon during a rehearsal for state competitions, one of the teenagers, a soon to be graduating senior, responded in anger when the director asked the "boys" to repeat their part and review their notes. This arrogant young man shot to his feet and refused until the director called him the "man" that he was. The director refused, although usually he would have simply said, "O.K. men, line 17." His point was that *men* would not need to tell another to call them that. As a group, the bass section walked out and destroyed our chances to place at the state competitions.

Most of us will immediately align with the choir director and support his decision not to give in to such defiance. However, the story does not end here. Mark knew the choir director very well, having babysat his son for many years. When he saw him a week or so later he confided in me that he should have handled it differently.

He told me that those boys needed choir more than choir needed them. We lived in a community with little to offer kids. It was during the drug epidemic of the early 1970s and this insightful teacher knew he was having a solid impact upon lives. He was a Christian who saw his occupation as his ministry.

A week or so later he called the boys back in and apologized to them in front of the choir. From then on he called them men. And, *wha-la*, they began acting like men and stopped their needling and disruption of class.

From this saint Mark learned some great lessons which have guided his ministry.

— The goal is more important than the road getting us there.

— The battles we win need to be worth winning.

— Apologizing is not a sign of weakness, but of strength.

Here are some red flags to consider in our ministries.

Having to be right. While right and wrong are certainly key concerns in training young people, it is easy to lose sight of the importance of our teaching relationship if we insist on always being right. Being right and teaching right from wrong are two very different issues, yet often assumed as the same.

As a high school student Mark was addicted to Bible study. He loved it and found solutions to problems in the words of our Lord. Mark studied the New Testament. One of his teachers found similar help in the Psalms. At that time in his life, though, Mark did not care much for the Psalms.

Personal preference differences happen all the time. However, the youth leader took this as a great offense and made it into what he believed was a spiritual issue. A battle ensued between Mark being fed from the New Testament and he being touched by the Old. Neither was right or wrong. Yet, that is what the disagreement turned into. Both were angry and felt slighted. Mark lost some respect for this leader and absented himself from church for a time. For his part, the teacher ignored his absence and never called.

Having to be "right" often sets the stage for losing the influence we have in the lives of our teens. If it is a non-issue, it is wise to allow them the space to become the person that Christ is making them. Refrain from taking a position on non-essentials. Keep that influence for things that are truly significant.

Trying to be "cool" or "hip." Nothing diminishes the effectiveness of our work more than when we try to become someone else; someone it is obvious we are not. The kids in our groups see our "transformation," take issue, and question our motivation. They need us to be who we are, and that is never to become one of them. Trying to be cool for their acceptance is unnecessary and usually embarrassing. In fact, one method of determining appropriate distance is in monitoring how often the kids tell you that you are "behind the times."

Wearing their clothes, listening to their music, crashing their personal events can cause resentment. They need us to be their *adult* leaders. They look to us for mature guidance and direction as they move into the next stages of their lives.

Granted, if you normally do things that they like, you shouldn't stop doing those things. Mark plays guitar and can hold his own with the best players in the youth group. That is part of who he is. But if he began wearing the styles they like to wear, he would become an obvious phony.

Personal inconsistencies. We, as leaders, are also in flux. We have not yet attained our final place of growth in Christ. Changes occur in our lives and with our families.

At times, these changes will affect our ministry. We may make bad decisions or be part of a problem. We may act inappropriately or say something in error. It happens.

When we fall short or fail, it is important to accept the action which will bring the best solutions. We are not talking of immorality issues, but rather at life issues, like a difficult time in our marriage, or the added stress if one of our own children runs into problems. It may be a personality conflict with another adult...or a teen; the daily conflicts of life which drain our energies or eat up our spare time.

When these seasons come our way, we need to be willing to step aside, take a breather, and put our houses in order. To give your students less is to deprive them of spiritual nurture.

However, if suitable, let the group or Sunday School class support you through your tough time. Ask the kids to step out and exercise their own prayer lives and help you. This is an opportunity to send the classroom home with them.

Unpreparedness. This is the trap that stalks us in our already too busy lives. Too often we walk into a classroom with no more than a glimmer of what we are going to do or say. Curriculum is an important assistant when teaching high schoolers. Yet, often the teachers merely glance at it and set forth to lead the class. This is unfair to the kids who come to learn God's Word and how they can apply it in their real-life situations from you.

It's true; things happen from time to time, and we find ourselves facing a class knowing in our hearts that there was not opportunity to fully prepare. But if these times become the norm, something is wrong or out of balance.

A wise step, for such occasions, would be to have a Plan B in hand, fully reviewed, and ready in advance. But treat your preparation time as holy time, a devotional period when you meet with God to talk to Him about your failures, His teens, and offer Him praise and thanksgiving.

Shooting from the hip. Similar to not being prepared is the shoot-from-the-hip tendency. This happens when the prepared plan is not followed in favor of something that spontaneously presents itself for discussion.

Teenagers have a natural ability to upset the apple cart. They devise tangents to take us off track from our prepared lesson plan. Early in Mark's ministry he discovered the kids were actively scheming to see how many weeks in a row they could get him off the topic in our curriculum. He fell for this mischievous game of theirs for weeks. An important unit on cults was largely demolished due to his inability to handle tangents and remain on track.

Occasionally, it is a great investment of class time to go with the flow of a related topic or something significant that occurred during the week. However, if the kids can derail us from sharing what they need to hear for a topic more interesting to them, they will.

Remain focused and only stray if the unplanned topic is of great advantage to the class as a "from the hip" spontaneous learning theme. Suggest the topic be added at the end of the unit or invite the interested kids to a separate gathering to fully discuss it.

Family constraints or personal obligations. If preparation time for your class becomes more and more difficult to carve out of each day due to family limitations or changes, or because of a change in your personal obligations, it's wise to pray about remaining the leader or teacher. Certainly, life changes often and rapidly in unexpected and unforeseen ways. If it changes in ways that are too pressing to give your class your best, then pray about taking a leave of absence or stepping aside. At a minimum, seek assistance from other adults in shoring up the class while you weather whatever storms you face.

This is only fair to you, to your changing situations or family, and to the kids who need leadership during these years.

Needing immediate gratification. We some-times need to know that our efforts are bearing fruit in the lives of our teenagers immediately. Here is your reality-based wake up call: *It doesn't happen very often.*

In many years of youth ministry Mark has seen that seeds of love, acceptance and under-standing planted today often do not return to him in fruit observed in the teenagers' lives. If seen, it usually doesn't come until much later. Some kids will never say "thanks" for the hours, the prayer, the time invested.

Look for feedback and affirmation of your efforts by what they do with their lives later. Accept your place in the lives of those kids who succeed in thriving careers, well balanced lives, and a continued walk in Christ. We, as youth workers, do something substantial and tangible. But expecting to see it today is asking a bit much.

Do not evaluate your ministry as teacher or leader based on the amounts of thanks or appreciation you receive. It is a faulty means of assessment. Rather, know that appreciation comes later when they see themselves successfully launched into living for Christ.

Looking for love, respect, or understanding. These are basic human needs, and we all seek them from our relationships. They are important kinds of feedback and entirely appropriate. Yet, trying to fulfill these needs through our young charges is seeking it from the wrong source. Far better to seek contentment from God.

In truth, the teenagers love you, but it is risky for them to show it. They respect you, but to let you know is deemed weak or uncool. They appreciate you for being there for them, but don't expect them to let an adult know they feel that way. They have not matured to that emotional point yet, and it is entirely foreign to most of them. They often do not see the importance in letting people know what they mean to them.

This is not meant to paint our youth in an unattractive light. It is simply who they are. Today's youth are often immature in interpersonal abilities. They are still being schooled; the foundation of their lives is still under construction. Ambivalent responses are all too normal for where they are in life. Later, during or after college, they may come back to visit you. That's when the feedback that matters will be offered.

Poor investment in your own spiritual life. Too often those of us in leadership think we can meet our personal spiritual needs through our study for classroom Bible studies. It is true that we learn and spend time with God and His word as we prepare for our lessons, but it may not be what God wants to tell you for your own life and growth in spiritual maturity.

It is essential that we allow ample time for our spiritual needs in addition to the time we spend in lesson preparation. An empty well cannot quench the thirst of the needy. We cannot give away what we do not possess.

Demanding our way or the highway. If we demand our own way for all things at all times, or else show the teenagers to the door with the "hit the road" comment, we set the stage for a roomful of hurting, disgruntled students. Our way cannot be assumed as being the only or best way. It is simply our way, our preference. That is not wrong. But neither should it be assumed to be right or the only right way.

Classroom time with high school students should have ample give and take. We all need to contribute and we all need to receive. In high school the kids begin to operate on a higher maturity level and enjoy thinking for themselves. High school-aged students want—and need to have—some input in the planning of the class. Wise teachers prepare for this exchange of ideas.

For example, you may prefer holding your youth programs in a youth room or classroom. It is likely easier for you. The supplies are all there and the room facilitates making the class time successful. Then, suddenly, Bob invites the whole group to his home next week for a more comfortable, homey setting. You can see the inconvenience, the forgotten materials, the transportation hassles, and you feel the urge to stifle the whole idea. Should a less than desirable idea from your viewpoint be assumed to be a flawed idea? Or does Bob's invitation hold some other merits and advantages?

Relinquishing our own way is a huge under-taking for some of us. We are used to being the boss. We may fear such actions compromise our authority and/or control over the class. Yet, many wonderful things may occur in Bob's living room that may never happen in the more formal classroom setting.

Most teens will know if they are not wanted. The message doesn't have to be spoken. But if one teen feels that way, then others may soon follow. Giving up our way is a healthy point of personal growth. The message becomes one of "give and take" rather than "my way only."

Insufficient personal spiritual support. As teachers or youth leaders it is essential that we preserve the awareness that we are part of a larger program within our local congregations. We, as teachers of the high school programs of our churches, are the tail end of the work done in the Children's and Youth departments of our churches. Many have invested in the kids prior to us and entrusted them and their spiritual development to our care. For our part, we will share with them and send them into the life of the larger church as adults.

It is tragic when a teacher cuts him or herself off from the support and care that the total Christian Education program can offer. Too often training events and spiritual growth opportunities for church school leaders are poorly attended. It saddens us. The Children's and Youth programs need to be a part of the "Big Picture" of the educational ministries of the local church.

Don't be a renegade. Participate in whatever supportive training your church leadership offers. If there is nothing currently available, volunteer to host the first gathering of teachers in your church for prayer and some staff training. Book studies or a monthly meal together to brainstorm and problem solve will only strengthen the whole church as you grow together as leaders. What a gift to your church family!

Hiding our differences. In most churches, the teachers are in touch with the goals and governing principles of the local congregation. It can be difficult and a huge disservice to the unity of the body when teachers and leaders hold different views on the church's doctrinal position.

For some unknown reason, we have seen this fairly often in youth ministry. Recently, Mark assisted a church that was having significant trouble with the high school youth leader. The root of the problems was that the youth leader held significantly different theological views from the pastor. We were not talking heresy by any means, however, the young people were confused by the differences in the Youth Group program and the pastor's sermons. Of course, the pastor was seen as "wrong" by the kids because he was "old" and "outdated." The youth leader insisted on sticking to his guns and caused quite a disruption to the work of the Lord in that church.

Sadly, the youth leader was aware of the differences prior to accepting the position with the church. He allowed his differences to remain hidden, only to emerge later in controversy and harm to the youth he genuinely wanted to serve. He was wrong to hide his true beliefs.

We see this more and more as youth leaders apply to churches for the job over the calling. If you, as leader of the high school youth in your church, are hiding differences in doctrine, theology, or personal belief from the pastor or governing board, request a meeting to see how these differences might be resolved before an explosion.

Distorted views of God. Each of us live lives filled with difficulty and trouble. While Jesus heals our aching hearts and restores us to fellowship, it is also true that the world may take its toll upon us in many ways.

If these traumas occur in our younger years, we often associate them with incorrect and distorted views of God. When no one is available to help us sort through these views and correct them, misconceptions and trouble may linger into adulthood and ministry.

If you were abused as a child, or had a parent who withheld affection or demanded perfection, you may have developed into an adult with the erroneous belief that God sees you likewise.

We have ministry friends who were treated badly by pastors or church leaders or who were raised with spiritual demands that could not be humanly met. Others had parents divorce or a parent die when they were young. Some have had God hand them a repeated "no" to their fervent prayer for a child and responded in bitterness to Him.

Examine your heart for any negative perceptions of the loving God of Scripture who sent His Son to pay the price for our salvation.

This is not necessarily a difficult thing to correct. Recognizing the distortion and comparing it to the God of the Bible is often all that needs to happen to adjust the misconception. It does not necessarily require a leave of absence or mark you for life as a bad teacher.

The problem is not in having a distorted image of God; it is in keeping one and passing it on to others through our teaching ministry.

Unable to be a team player. We were part of a team meeting with some of our upper elementary Sunday School teachers. We stressed that we were a unit in our work with the children and the youth of our church. We communicate the life and work of Jesus Christ in a continuum of ministry that begins at the birth of each child and travels with them through life to the grave. No other institution has the access we have as the church. From birth to death we touch lives.

In this meeting we emphasized to these elementary teachers how important they are as links in the lives of these children who will be soon heading into the junior high program and then senior high. They begin the work that the upper age group teachers will build upon for many tomorrows.

Occasionally a teacher wants to do it all their way. They don't want to use the curriculum. They want to teach the things they believe are important. A personal agenda battles against the larger plan of the local church. Certainly some initiative and leadership is a wonderful characteristic, as is adapting a lesson to our ministry gifts. Yet, when overdone, it can be detrimental to the larger efforts of team ministry.

Think about how impressive it is for children to see that the church has relevant programs for them across the lifespan. There can always be something to which they may look with excitement and anticipation. The younger kids look ahead to where they are going, and the older kids look back at all they have learned. Adults use this knowledge as the foundation and springboard into deeper maturity in Christ. Our kids grow up influenced and touched by our ministries, strong in their commitment to continued church attendance as adults.

Think About You

Why are you a high school teacher or youth leader? What will this ministry provide for you? What baggage do you need to unpack in order to be more effective? What are your needs?

Whatever your personal need to be teacher, allow yourself to be a learner. Be teachable. The teens have much to share with you about life and spiritual awareness. It is an interesting blessing of our work.

None of us has lived in the world of the teenagers in your class. Life is different for them than it was for us. Through listening we learn of their trials. Through their stories and their questions we learn how they feel. They encourage us as they tell of the ways they have applied their faith in their day-to-day living. Just as God is there for us, God is there for the kids. Our part is to help them know what God is like and how they can hear His voice. What an awesome privilege!

5 *Ready to Teach?*

About 19 million parents have brought close to 22 million teenagers, ages 13 to 18, into United States junior and senior high schools. While the lower grades are not within our focus, they are an important consideration because they soon will be sitting in our high school classes.

Let's imagine the program year is about to begin. You've been accepted as a teacher, met with your department leaders, received some training or orientation, and reviewed the curriculum for your high school class or youth group. You've prayed and are ready to teach.

With your hand on the door knob, Bible and other materials under your arm, you walk in and greet the circle of students with whom you will spend an hour or so each week in this room. Other than their names, what do you really know about them as a group? What is their world like? How do you understand life, faith, and God? What drives them? What do you expect of you? And you of them? What wakes them up in the night? What motivates them in the day? And, perhaps most importantly, how can you best communicate Jesus Christ to them in a personally challenging and genuine way?

While the age and grade differences are certainly influenced through the various developmental issues, there are specific and identifiable trends, tendencies, issues, and attitudes prevalent in today's high schoolers that you need to understand as part of your preparation as leader or teacher. These will affect your relationships with them both in and out of the classroom setting.

To be prepared, you need to consider the extremes in the words of Jesus when he suggests we be, "wise as serpents, harmless as doves" (Matthew 10:16). The serpent brings to us images of silent aggression, crafty awareness, and patience to capture its prey. The dove speaks to us of peace, confidence, and a nature of trust and gentleness. The Hebrew mind would understand that these were examples from nature which speak to us symbolically of good attributes in our daily lives. As a teacher, they provide us with an awareness of the range of skills needed to minister effectively with and to today's youth—craft and caring.

Each teenager in your class is a special creation fashioned with love made as only God can make us. Although unique as individuals, as a group they will exhibit some general characteristics.

It is fair to say that today's teenagers approach life thoughtfully and earnestly with both of their eyes wide open, observing life as it unfolds around them. Many times, what they see is very different from what we see. There is a gulf between us, as adult leaders, and them, as inexperienced youth. We become a source of understanding *for* them only if we have an understanding *of* them.

George Barna, an astute observer of Christian and secular culture, identifies what he calls the "Six S's." In his excellent presentation of high school students at the end of this century and into the beginning of the next, he finds their attitudes cluster in six categories:

- Serious
- Stressed out
- Self-reliant
- Skeptical
- Spiritual
- Survivors

Before we examine these categories, let's remember a bit about their world and what it would feel to be a young person facing the slim promises of a life influenced by:

- a divorce rate approaching 60%
- innumerable questions and confusing issues
- many fears coupled with inadequate maturity and knowledge
- rapidly changing technologies
- uncertain economics and an uncertain future
- AIDS and other STDs
- revisionist history and political correctness
- increasing drug and alcohol abuses
- the possibility that they will not attain or exceed their parents' financial securities
- multi-cultural, secular influences on faith
- life as presented by such sources as MTV and sitcoms
- unbalanced, biased media presentations of our world, and lots more.

Consider how many of these dynamics were not factors in our own teenage years. Life has certainly changed, but has it changed for the better when it comes to our kids?

Barna's research offers us some solid guidance in understanding the world of our high school students. Through the challenges and insights of his "Six S's" we can better grasp how they perceive life.

Youth today are:

Serious about life and the issues they face daily. They see their world and the potential or real impacts of outcomes which are linked to such problems as morality, racism, politics, education, economics, and the like. While uncertain as to how they might deal with these and other issues, they exhibit an awareness of them often unprecedented by earlier generations. They are serious about what life means and how they might make it better.

Youth today are:

Stressed Out from the issues like those above. They have discovered that life can be difficult, especially when the more immediate issues of their day-to-day life are also considered. Contributing issues such as family disintegration, ever shifting social values, school expectations, dating and relationships, crime, and their budding sexuality may add further to their feelings of being overwhelmed. To them, stress and life are synonymous.

Youth today have:

Self-reliant feelings which feed their desire to be independent. Their personal sense of unencumbered freedom is a major force in our youth. They know so much and have experienced so much that it is hard to convince them that they need limits and boundaries.

Youth today are:

Skeptical about life and the two worlds in which they exist —the secular and the sacred. This is another defining notion of our young people. Trust of adults, leaders, and role models is no longer a given for them. They pose questions from a negative perception based in claims which seem too good to be possible. Too many promises have not been kept for them to simply accept things by blind faith.

Youth today are:

Spiritual in a deeply searching sense which, unfortunately, often encompasses any available spiritual position or trend. Even church kids wear New Age crystals and make calls to the psychic phone services. They seek direction and strive for spiritual meaning with little discrimination for the source.

Youth today are:

Survivors of the numerous obstacles and challenges before them. They seek a better understanding and a more positive world view. Their lives are discouraging on many fronts. Yet, they find meaning and develop functional ways to overcome with an inspiring ability to make life work.

At this point the temptation is in all our minds to scream, "How negative can you be!" However, it is a different world than it was in our day. It is faster, swiftly changing, and, in too many arenas, it is racing to destruction. The evening news overwhelms our adult ability to mediate the punches life throws our way. Teens watch the same news with few of the adult coping skills.

As adult leaders with a knowledge of God's Word guiding our ability to share the answers to these problems, we must be aware that these kids are growing up all too fast and provide the help they need to moderate the incredible amounts of "real life" they face. We cannot teach or lead from the comfort zone of how we learned and how life was for us as teens. It is truly a different world. We must recognize how this world is for these kids and give them biblical coping skills and truth.

Barna's Six S's provide us with a surprisingly complete and insightful means of summing up the ways these influences which are pressed upon our teenagers have given birth to outcomes which describe them so well.

Glancing around your classroom at your assembled students might invite you to remember your teenage years. Those of us who are Baby Boomers will remember fearing nuclear holocaust and not wanting to go to war. Sexual freedom and promiscuous immorality worked to destroy the moral structure of our generation. Our lives seemed to be dedicated to challenging the values and laws of our nation. Additionally, we were the folks who experimented with almost any substance, considered any philosophy regardless of its effect upon society, and turned upon our leaders simply for the sake of questioning.

Older adults, or those who are grandparents to today's teenagers, were formed in all developmental areas by such forces as nationally supported wars, the days before TV took its place of central dominance in our homes, a stronger feeling of what America was and is, and far more intact families, many of which were extended to include their grandparents. More than half lived on family farms in a rural setting, enjoying a quieter life and were blessed with the family working as a unit for a common goal.

Farm life meant responsibility. An extended family meant parenting relief and support, and the buffer of older, wiser grandparents assisting in communicating values to the children. An absence of TV meant quiet evenings of family interaction and meals prepared and eaten together. Church was often seen as a friendly and joyous family activity. Conversation was an honored art. Even casual reflection on these changes will underscore how different life is among today's high school youth.

And yet, as teacher and leader, you are poised to empower each student with the timeless good news of Jesus Christ. The world is constantly changing with fearful statistics and gruesome news accounts, but it is our privilege to teach the absolutes the world would deny. This is where we can change the world, by giving kids the certainty of moral absolutes of right and wrong as well as an unchanging Source of answers to every question.

It may seem hopeless at times, but hope is inherent to the message you bring these students sitting before you in class. Your personal relationship with Christ, the targeted goals of your curriculum, the life application of God's truths will influence the lives of those to whom you minister.

Consider these additional thoughts as you begin your ministry.

Change is inevitable. It occurs with each new generation. It is part of life, and although your world and circumstances are not as theirs is, your internalized lessons about life can be used to guide them in their changing world.

The value of your presence will exceed their suspicion of older persons. Studies maintain that while peer influences are still a major force upon teens, it does not replace or undermine the investments of respected adults into their lives.

Teenagers seek a life model of balance and structure into which they might pour the conflicting and often overwhelming aspects of their lives. Jesus Christ is that life model. Your task, in part, is to make Christ relevant to their lives. Never underestimate the impact of your work with them.

So while everything is different, there is still a constant, a thread which enables your ministry. All-in-all, things are the same as they were from the beginning. Men and women growing up in trouble and struggle, challenged by life and dark forces, find both joy and disaster, and need a Savior to return them to God. This was the same for us as it is today for the youth in your classroom.

While there are many valid criticisms of the African proverb, "It takes a village to raise a child," there is some truth in it for us. Because we are the body of Christ, God expects us to work together for each other—the children in the pre-school area, the elementary kids, the young people and the adults each bring something to the church that enriches and helps each of us to grow up together in Christ. Mom and dad can't do it alone. School teachers and coaches can't do it alone. Pastors, Sunday School teachers, and youth leaders can't do it alone. Nor can the police, bosses, music instructors or all the other adults touching the lives of our children. We work together to direct young men and women bursting with the holy potential God places within them. God needs you and all that you do to bring forth the harvest.

What a great reason to teach our youth.

6 *Teens and Programming*

Teenagers support programs in which they feel some involvement. Success is insured by allowing them the opportunity to be an active part in deciding, planning, and executing any program, be it a mission trip, a special speaker, or the activities. They support what they own.

We both remember our efforts to give our youth group kids the freedom to determine some of their own Bible studies.

In youth group the kids *always* selected topics or events which were fun and interesting to them. There is nothing wrong with fun or interesting. However, when the topics requested were only about dating, sex, music, friendship, and teenager problems, and the events were only amusement parks, canoeing, adventures, and play time, we could see that a deficiency in spiritual nourishment was going to take place.

What a young adult wants and what a young adult needs are two very different areas which require leadership wisdom to moderate. This is an important part of being a teacher or leader in the church youth programs. Our kids trust us and look to us for a balanced spiritual diet. They are not sophisticated enough to decide for themselves, so we need to adapt their suggestions as programs are charted.

We all know what a shopping trip for groceries would look like if we gave our kids $150.00 and said, "You shop for the week and I'll push the cart." Mountains of sugared cereal, every soda imaginable, chips, pretzels, frozen pizza, a tub of peanut butter, and some selections from the candy aisle would only be the beginning. While these treats are fine upon occasion, they do not constitute a well-balanced diet that promotes growth or healthy physical development. That's why we let them push the cart and we shop.

The same holds true in programming for our teenagers in the church. They will ask for programs and lessons on very important topics, like those mentioned above, but a diet of those programs exclusively will not insure healthy spiritual development. Few teenagers would request a study on doctrines like justification or redemption. End times they like, the teaching about missions—they aren't so sure. Mixing the subjects they request with the ones we feel are crucial promotes the relationship between leaders and students. It also provides the well-rounded spiritual diet that fosters healthy relationships between students, leaders, and God.

Kids need the basic "rights" of being allowed to make mistakes and fail. Almost all of the New Testament teaches us that spiritual growth is developed, at least in part, through interacting with the events life gives us from a godly perspective. As Christians, we understand that those lessons are not just chance occurrences, but the guiding hand of God gently pushing us into, and out of, learning experiences. Certainly, we get ourselves into jams often enough. Yet, we have all found ourselves in situations that could only be God's immersion in purifying fire.

Teenagers need the same freedom to experience first hand that God is there for them and that ministry does not just happen. Sunday School, youth group, mission trips, work camps, summer church camp, youth clubs, and all the other teaching opportunities we may find ourselves leading take lots of planning, praying, and laboring. Since these all take time and energy, why not insure better support and success from the youth to whom they are aimed by enlisting them into the process?

Just last week two teenage girls came to Mark asking that he plan a special summer fun trip to a local amusement park, tying it in with a planned overnight retreat. He said it sounded like a great idea. Would they help plan it and take the responsibility for the trip?

They wanted to know what that meant. Mark listed picking the date, setting the budget, planning meals, deciding where we would stay, contacting other advisors, etc. Wide eyed they refused—immediately. "That's your job," one of them offered.

Mark gently reminded them that his job was to help them become the persons God intended them to be. He volunteered his assistance and experience, but declined to do it for them. He suggested they think about it.

An hour or so later they approached him again, still not volunteering, but asking a few more detailed questions. On the trip home from the soup kitchen we had just served in, they said that all of this surprised them, but they thought they might like to try planning the trip after all.

Now, the fact is that he could plan this trip better, faster, with fewer meetings, and it would be a great success, but nothing would be gained except a fun trip with the youth of the church. However, by enlisting the two young women, he'll be investing in leadership for the next three years they remain in the high school group and promote their individual successes as they see what they can do to serve God and others in a secure environment where failure will not be fatal. The following summer, when a trip is offered again, these leaders likely will step forward to plan it.

Your teenagers need you to make them aware of their own spiritual gifts in leadership, planning, and "pulling off" what they programmed. Share the group with the group.

We both have used youth leadership in our church work. In Mark's youth groups, teen leadership teams work side by side with the advisors to put together nearly every aspect of our entire program. The kids pick the topics, get some of the speakers, choose the songs, research the games, and do some of the scheduling. They also share in the success of a job well done.

Years ago we became convinced that summer work camp experiences underline and emphasize what Scripture teaches about serving and helping others. We initially decided that the easy way to do this was to plug into existing groups, like Habitat for Humanity, and building housing for needy folks.

However, while Habitat is an excellent program, the particular work site we selected would not let the kids do any of the building. Rather, they gave the kids bags and asked them to pick up garbage, or pile the scrap lumber, or rake some leaves. The kids did the work in the right spirit of helping others, but they were looking with great desire at the house being erected before their eyes. They came to pound nails and to saw 2x4s. One fellow told them that the trash needed to be picked up and that job was as important as the building, but no one was very convinced. If the trash was so important, why were none of the adults picking it up?

We decided that the kids could be taught to rebuild or repair most any common problem. So, we began looking for a work camp opportunity that would let high school Christians show their servanthood by changing the living conditions of a poor or needy family. In the past decade we have taken hundreds of kids to job sites to roof, side, paint, repair, and build themselves. And, they also pick up the trash.

They have loved the work recipients, sharing openly that they were there because Christ loved them. They have raised their own support, given up a week of summer vacation, and cooked their own meals, often sleeping on church basement floors. During the evenings, as we soaked sore feet or applied sunburn cream, we have talked about Christ's love, studying the Bible as our guide for the work camp. Not the standard view of today's youth.

Teenagers need us, as their leaders, to plan for the kinds of deficiencies which are evident in their lives. Their culture, as most of our adult culture, usually seeks to be a part of the cool, the hip, the fun. Just as our mothers made us eat good food and take our vitamins, so must we, as youth teachers and leaders, help them swallow the spiritual vitamins needed for a healthy faith. We have a responsibility to give them ways to overcome those deficiencies.

As you can tell, this isn't a chapter about how to plan a retreat, favorite foods to include at the hay ride, or what kinds of activities kids will most likely support enthusiastically making us as leaders look good. No. It is a chapter on *why* we program. Do you look at the underlying spiritual growth each activity offers the kids in your group? Do you plan ways to emphasize spiritual growth and pleasing God into your programs?

Remember, teens support programs which they own. They gain ownership when they feel involved. Allow them the opportunity to be an active part in deciding, planning, and executing any program or activity. Involve them in the Sunday morning lesson planning and carry through. Give them responsibilities in the weekly Bible study groups. Help them learn why the lessons follow a particular plan. Give them time and ways to grow up as well as the freedom to fail.

Active, hands-on programming teaches many spiritual growth issues and truths—and facilitating this makes you an active participant in the formation of their desire to be involved in the work of Christ.

7 Critical Elements of Teaching

The fact is that we are "employed" by God through the ministry of the local church to lead kids into a relationship with Jesus Christ that is both life-changing and eternal. Our calling is a precious stewardship that gives us meaning and purpose in our own walk with Christ.

This chapter examines some of the strategies which make teaching high schoolers more successful and comprehensive. Our teaching and leadership ministries need to be approached professionally and with an attitude that reflects the very best of God for our students.

Sociologists and psychologists tell us that the years between 15 and 25 comprise a decade of decision which will largely direct the choices, values, and direction of the rest of a person's life. Most people are saved before the age of 18. Junior high and senior high years produce decisions for Christ which are more likely to be kept through the life span.

In one way or another, we will sow in their lives by virtue of our position. If we sow sparingly or use less than excellent seed, we will not make much impact. And, we will lose the blessing of being His instrument to shape their lives toward a realization of their lifelong, full-time service for Him.

However, if we tackle the challenge with excellent preparation and follow through, we can watch our investment in their lives increase year after year. Excellence does not just happen; there is a "why" which is answered by treating Christian education as the trowel which places the mortar between the bricks of what God has for these young adults. If our teens are to be equipped to stand for Christ against the trends and pressures of their world, we must apply the Word of God carefully, thoroughly, excellently in their lives.

Much of the information coming from secular educational research these days is very useful to our work. At times we have to reinterpret the data within the framework of our faith, but it seems we have to do that much of the time anyway! Such was the challenge of the early church as it reclaimed pagan holidays for Christ by putting a Christian understanding to horribly decadent practices. Rather than completely eliminate or ignore the celebrations, our spiritual forefathers simply replaced the worldly with Christ. That's why we have Christmas on December 25.

As you face your high schoolers, approach them with an understanding of how each of the various aspects of your teaching program affects them and the effectiveness of your ministry.

Look at:
• You as the teacher
• The class as a whole
• Each individual making up your class
• The curriculum used by your church

• The room in which you meet

• Unplanned changes or adjustments (such as the presence of a visitor or some event in the life of your church or community)

• What is necessary for the day

Each of these dynamics, and likely some we do not note, will either add to or detract to the work which is done in the classroom. Let's examine each one.

You as teacher. How do you feel about teaching today? Is all well at home? On the job? With your family? What spiritual growth have you seen in your life this week? How did you cope with failure, disappointment, fear—and success? In other words, do not minimize your place in the teaching package; make necessary adjustments as required. God did not make you to be a "teaching machine." Part of your effectiveness is wrapped up in the accepting of yourself as a living, feeling person. Do not try to dismiss your "stuff" or your "baggage." Denial will not help you be yourself. And being yourself is a critical ingredient to having your class accept you.

Your class as a whole. Every class develops its own, individual dynamic. Become aware of the "feel" of your class and compensate as needed. For example, does your class take the teaching time seriously or do they "cut up"? Are there many students with learning problems? Has this group of kids been together for a long time? Are there new kids?

Dynamics are not set in stone and may fluctuate from week to week. Personalities will influence and cause unfavorable outcomes. For example, the kid who is forced to attend is almost always a problem. Preachers' kids can be a challenge. If a student tries to thwart your lesson through intellectualizing what can be understood only through the eyes of faith, it may be a tough session. All of these mishaps can keep us awake on Saturday night with apprehension for the Sunday morning class.

The personality of the class is there. Can you recognize it? It will somehow be reflected in the teaching process and needs to be addressed. Success and how much of God's Word the class studies will be determined by how well you discern that personality and adjust to meet its needs.

Each individual student. The group will reflect each of its parts. Try to meet some of the needs of each group member. For example, recently we have found an increased number of children of divorce in our youth group, as well as in our Sunday School program. We have needed to face that dynamic and accommodate for these individuals in other ways, like personal counseling, rewording the material in our lessons in reference to family to include the single parent family, and discouraging any negative comments from other teenagers.

Curriculum. These lesson materials are so important to the success of the class. These guidebooks insure your chances of success by providing you with the information needed to accomplish sound educational goals which build upon each other week after week. You cannot function competently if you pull a lesson out and look at it for 20 minutes on Saturday night. Nor will it work as designed if you skim it for the first time while trying to communicate it to the class. You owe it to the class and to the God you serve to be well-prepared.

In the first three weeks of a new quarter, examine the curriculum and the class together. These may be awkward weeks as the needs of the students meet the strengths and messages of the material. Use these weeks to gain a feel for both and then begin adjusting and fine tuning to provide the best class sessions possible. Make use of ongoing evaluations by thinking through this week's class before next week's presentation. What worked? What could have gone better? What application questions or activities do you need to add to address the issues your teens raise? Then, make some changes.

Your Classroom. We often lament at the state of our classrooms. The room environment and setting is essential in high school educational ministry.

High schoolers need to "mark" their part of the world. Their rooms at home reflect who they are, their opinions, their world view, their hopes and dreams, and their fears. Give the teenagers the time and materials needed to decorate the Sunday School and/or youth room to fit them, their life, and their faith. Ask the kids how to transform this room into a learning space which welcomes them.

Are you on chairs around tables? Would a circle of sofas or bean bag chairs work better? If a lesson will be reflected through art work, do you have the space for the kids to work? Are there teen chosen posters either from your curriculum or from a Christian bookstore? How can the room become a "hook" to the students? Remember, kids support what they feel they have invested in.

In one Sunday School room in which Mark taught some legendarily rambunctious high schoolers, we decided to hang Poster Diaries around the room. A Poster Diary is a large sheet of posterboard which is hung on the wall and identified by a simple name tag, one poster for each student.

Each week the teenagers came to class with physical symbols of what they had been doing during the week. One would bring her number from a 10K track race and tape it to her board. Others brought concert ticket stubs. Class pictures were added or pictures of friends. Some put Scripture verses they discovered in their devotional time. A pressed flower went up in memory of a grandmother who died. Preceding each addition of the symbols to the students' board, we gave each student time to tell what happened. This brief and simple addition brought new life to our class and a new feeling of attachment to the room and to each other.

This kind of investment isn't about money. It's about communicating an inviting level of comfort to the whole class which is "lived out" on the walls of the room. Inexpensive is just fine with the kids, as long as it is *them* expressed in the room. And each Fall, re-evaluate the room. As new kids join the group, the dynamics and personal expressions may change.

Unplanned changes or adjustments. It is important to address the things that have occurred in the week between classes if they are even slightly monumental. If a student dies at school in a car wreck, or someone they know has attempted suicide, or a mother has died, or the school team went down in ignominious defeat, spend a moment to talk about it. These events in the lives of the community or the kids will be on their minds. It is a work of grace to incorporate these events, changes, or adjustments into the ministry of the classroom. It brings real life into the realm of the gospel and shows teens that the spiritual and the secular cannot be separated. Each affects the other.

A visitor can affect the course of the time together, so take a few moments to introduce and learn a bit about any newcomers. But reduce their anxiety by not putting them on the spot. The class is more likely to accept the visitor if they have an opportunity to learn something about the person.

What is necessary for the day. What important events, such as a birthday, a holiday, or the anniversary of some important event in your church or community, have occurred? Take a few moments to work these affairs into the class. It makes the time together more friendly.

Also, if something is happening in the life of the church, such as the departure of a pastor, entering a new building, or some special observance, talk about it in class.

These kinds of considerations make a difference in our work. Some students will be more sensitive; others almost oblivious. However, in addressing these dynamics, we make our teaching more relevant. Remember, kids reject what they feel is not an important part of their lives. Involve them in the life of the church and with each other.

The Critical Elements

Some strong factors influence the success of teaching high schoolers in the Sunday School or youth programs. They tend to reflect where they are in their development and perceptions, thus making them essential components to your overall presentation.

These considerations are mostly common sense in nature. Try a new one, or review one already learned, every week.

Age Appropriate. Mark remembers attending a curriculum review program and being shocked in two ways. One curriculum, which our church had planned to purchase, was way too immature for the kids in the high school class. To buy it would be to insure a year of lesson ridicule and poor attention. Turning to another packet, it seemed the intended audience must have been brain surgeons or rocket scientists. Seminary education would have been needed to learn the lessons.

You know your kids better than anyone. Make sure the curriculum chosen, the way you present it, and the discussions reflect the age of the students. High schoolers will "tune out" if the level of the class is considered too childish. They will "pick it apart" if it is too sophisticated. The wish to learn, in most cases, is present in every class, but the materials have to make sense. You need to be able to make the connections between the material and the student.

Reality-Based. Again we come to that essential element of working with high schoolers. They simply insist that the material in the lesson make sense, in some way, to their place in life. If it does not, today's teenager will reject the lesson. The danger is, of course, that they will also reject God's Word as being irrelevant.

Sometimes you'll get the sense in the course of the lesson that the kids have disconnected. This is no reason to abandon ship and go to some alternative lesson. Rather, shift your presentation by applying the material to something in your life, or in their lives, or to some event in the community. Usually the problem is not in the content of the material being presented. Make the application and the examples relevant to what they are facing. Insert a different interface which allows for the application of the material.

Biblically Sound with Godly Tolerance. Kids today will support the underdog, even if the underdog is wrong. We have seen teenagers take the side of the sinner being used as an example because the material describing it became too personal or intolerant. When Jesus confronted the woman taken in adultery, He did not call her bad names or make fun of her. He told her to stop the behavior and forgave her. He expected better of her than she did of herself.

I have seen leaders ridicule and malign sinful people, only to have it blow up in their faces because the kids took the side of the sinner. Kids identify with the "bad guy" because they are often so aware of their own shortcomings. They want us, as leaders, to condemn the sin biblically without labeling the the person in question as "good or bad."

Kids do better if allowed to criticize the *actions* of a peer. Let them discuss it openly and you'll fare better. If you present the issue by putting down the underdog, rather than deploring the sin, you may flop.

Interesting and Challenging. Adults sometimes miss what is interesting or challenging to teenagers because we base the assessment on our own lives. We have seen nationally recognized speakers, gifted women and men, who did not come through because they shared their messages within the framework of what adults find interesting or challenging.

Interest is based upon "buy in" to the material. The lesson should sing with relevance and personal application. Or, it should address a question that has been previously unanswered. To meet the element of challenge, the lesson has to take the student just a bit beyond where they want to go. It has to appeal to or fascinate them on some level. If the lesson misses these two elements, it will predictably flounder.

Active Learning with Discovery. Active learning involves the student in manipulating the lesson content or truths in different forms. It involves motions or storytelling or art. The key is that the learner interacts with the lesson on some level other than just reading the words.

The key to successful active learning is that it leads the student to some kind of discovery. Maybe it is discovering how Christ's life and ministry is enacted in the church today. Or perhaps it opens up an area of study that enhances the material of the lesson, like visiting a museum display of daily living in Bible times. When discovery is involved, the learning accomplished is more than facts, it is life changing. The chapter on "Adapting A Topic" gives more tips on active learning.

Bring the Student into a Greater Passion for Christ. We are called to increase the knowledge of Jesus Christ to each of the students in our class. Each student is a gift from God entrusted into our care and guidance. However, ask yourself: Does the lesson being taught make them feel more passionate or closer to God?

We cannot teach a love for God. It has to come from within the learner. Yet, our testimony, or the testimony of others, is a sure way to take the "black on white" words of the lesson and bring them to life, illustrating how it can work for another.

Testimony is far more than the stories of our sin and salvation. It is the current accounting of how God is working in our lives on a daily basis.

Testimony in our day has disintegrated to a person's story of how God rescued him or her from the clutches of Satan and delivered them into God's caring grip. This form of testimony is only a tiny portion of what God has done or is doing in our lives.

A lesson on forgiveness will be personalized and internalized if someone in your church forgave someone who wronged them and will share their story.

A lesson on God's call will be more productive if someone other than a pastor or missionary can share how God led their lives into some wonderful work. These stories from regular, simple, everyday people give hope to a young person. Most teens believe that they are the exception to every spiritual blessing. Stories which confirm God's work in our lives help them believe that they, too, will find God's hand directing them along their way. Such assurances increase the passion we all want to have for God.

Community Building. Our life in Christ, while personal, is designed and intended to be shared with the greater community of believers, in our class, our church, and in our world. Make appropriate additions to incorporate the relationship we have with other Christians.

Our church works closely with a small inner-city church in metropolitan Cleveland. It is a depressed area of poverty and great need. There are homeless families and more nightmare stories than can be imagined. Yet, we link forces with that small church to bring the message of Christ's love to the community. Lives are being changed through Christ and our work. These lessons would not normally be learned in our town. But through our relationship with this church, a strong sense of community in Christ is built.

Community also occurs within the group. We recommend playing brief community-building games periodically to increase the level of shared relationships in the group. A number of good books are available which outline such activities. However, one that never seems to grow old is to pair off the kids with someone they don't know well and have them make a list of all the things they have in common. Do not allow them to list things like two eyes, two ears. Instead, ask them to talk and find out what hobbies, books, classes, friends, etc. they both enjoy. Or, they can focus on things they don't like such as a rival sport team, a particular class, a time of the day, etc. then tally up who had the most in common among the pairs in the room.

Relationship Building. While similar to building community, relationship building is different in that it allows opportunity for the individuals in the class to work together in ways that make them closer. Community addresses the entire group, while relationship building strengthens the participants of the class in personally shared bonds.

Just as our relationship with Christ is a one-on-one relationship that is developed over time, so must our relationships within the group be nurtured on a regular basis. The teenagers in your youth group or class need to have some familiarity with each other in order to work and grow together in Christ.

This is especially important for groups that consistently number over 25 to 30 kids per week.

Close relationships get stalled when a group exceeds 20 persons, so effort must be made to break the larger group into smaller groups where each can learn more about others.

One easy way is to incorporate 10 minutes or so of small group discussion into many meetings. We like to use groups of no more than eight teenagers and, when possible, we have an adult advisor sit in each group to moderate and keep things on track. If you offer no agenda other than "talk about today's lesson," the time will move into current sports scores or what the new principal at school is like. Give them three general questions about the topic to discuss. They will do very well in learning about one another if given the time. In the long run of the group, these relationship building activities pay huge dividends.

Self-Awareness Building. One of the age-old questions of teenagers is, "Who am I?" They struggle in their identity as they seek to find meaning in their lives. Helping them find themselves in Christ is a vital contribution to their spiritual growth. For, if left to themselves or the world, they will not formulate the kinds of understandings of themselves that are consistent with the character of Christ.

In our teaching and leadership ministries we need to investigate life beyond our own tiny circle. In other words, it is critical that we get beyond our own calling in Christ and allow the larger world of serving God to be explored.

Certainly pastors and missionaries are to be esteemed for their service to the body of Christ, but help students to understand the ministry contributions that God expects of the rest of us. The understanding that God calls each of us to full-time ministry in every occupation and area of life is an important seed to plant in the high school years.

Only a few are called to serve as pastors and missionaries. Every believer is called to full-time service whether as a plumber who gives honest work or a doctor who helps patients seek the only Source of true healing. This is a gift you can give each student in each youth group through each year of your ministry. Explore this truth by sharing with the class many forms and functions of Christian service, from mission work to an assembly line. Testimonies will certainly increase the impact of this lesson. God needs people in every area of work and public service.

Integrating Teenagers with and without Church Backgrounds. A child of any age can feel uncomfortable when she or he is suddenly "thrust" into a Sunday School or youth group setting. Whatever the reason, the new student with no church background is in culture shock and very uncomfortable. Our Christian terms don't make sense. Turning to a Bible verse is like trying to decipher a foreign language. How to act, behave, pray, and worship may all be very new.

When a student comes your way with no church background, or even one different from your own, work to make the visit easier by spending some extra time defining the why and what of the lesson.

Do not assume they understand. Better to assume they do not and make provisions.

The benefit to the student is obvious. However, there is an additional benefit that the regular class may learn—how to be hospitable to others in the name of Christ. Showing love, concern, and care to strangers is expected of the believer. Modeling this in class helps every student learn.

Promoting Biblical Values. Our lessons are filled with Bible-based values which underline how we should live for Christ. However, an important element in our teaching time is to make sure that the lesson's values are understood by each student. As the culture of the world so strongly opposes the values of Christ, we must take extra time to evaluate if the kids are "getting it."

We have been quite amazed to find that some of our high schoolers over the years acted out against Christian values because they misunderstood what the Bible taught. Just because the lesson is taught, it is no proof that the teenagers heard it. Draw the value out for them plainly and allow them time to interact with it. Usually they appropriate the value into their lives after a bit of challenge and a few questions.

Some other considerations

As you pursue your desire to be the very best high school teacher or leader you can be, continue to look at your style of lesson presentation critically and honestly. We all need to upgrade our skills and abilities. Here are some additional tips to developing excellence.

• *People retain what they "own."* Both the teacher and the student will do better if they genuinely own the material. This means that the subject under study has been stretched, and examined, and thought about, and chewed on, and looked at from all angles to the place where the information is a part of our lives. When we wrestle with it, we discover the ins and outs of the subject's application in our lives.

A model, known as Bloom's Taxonomy, was proposed for educational purposes. It examines the normal and natural steps of successful learning as a process which, once completed, will fit together as a whole. The model covers *comprehension, application, analysis, synthesis, and evaluation.*

In **comprehension** the goal is to understand what is being taught or said. Is it clear? Is it learned as it taught? The attention from you, as teacher, toward the student seeks to assess if each learner has received the knowledge of what the information says in its basic form. This makes the knowledge something which may be personally acquired.

After it is understood for its facts, the information is then applied to the life or circumstances of the learner. This step of **application** shifts impersonal information into something which has some relevance in the high schooler's daily life or experiences.

Next the lesson is **analyzed** for any inconsistencies. This is human nature and common. Expect that the students may try to reject what they are learning at this stage as they put it under the microscope. If the fact was perceived accurately in step one, and has some place of relevancy in step two, then the fact will survive the step of analysis. If it does not survive, then something in one or two needs attention.

In *synthesis*, the learned information is related to other aspects of the person's life and experience. It gets "cross referenced" to other and different ways the lesson may be applied. Synthesis is important in that it helps us use what we learn in church in situations outside of the church. A teenager may learn how we behave as Christians in church camp, only to fail to use the information at school. Synthesis takes the church camp lesson back to school.

Finally, *evaluation* occurs as the person decides how this information will become an active part of their life. Using the information beyond the classroom happens when evaluation is successful.

Bloom's Taxonomy is a useful tool for following the element of "what is learned" into the goal of "what is lived." We all know of times in our own lives when we learned the facts of a lesson and neglected to follow through on the application. Christianity is not about living facts, it is about applying these facts on a daily basis in all that we do and think. It is the putting on of Jesus' new nature in our lives as we put off our old nature. We cannot factually overcome sinful behavior. We must put the behavior off, by applying the new behaviors we learn. This is what ownership of a lesson means.

• *Support Materials.* Older, larger congregations may have boxes of costumes, props, left over resources and the like for adding support to a lesson. Younger, smaller churches may be working with bare bones resources and unable to offer much in the way of frills. Whatever your situation, use support materials in ways that spark the imagination and make the lessons real.

In one church the teachers annually develop a time line of the Old Testament using the walls as their visual support. Each summer the room is repainted. Each fall, winter and spring, as the Old Testament time line is studied and learned, the class paints the focus scenes of the lessons on the wall to show how the Old Testament unfolded. It is an inexpensive way to involved the teenagers in the production of the Old Testament as they are studying it.

Most curricula offers ideas to support a lesson. These may be as important as the lesson itself for we are teaching the TV generation.

To be honest, we must acknowledge that what Hollywood does reaches teens much better visually and creatively. If we bore the students, we lose them. So imagine how this week's lesson can spring off of the page and into the minds and hearts of your class, then make it so!

Lesson Wreckers

Lesson wreckers are those students or situations which arise in the course of a lesson which either throw it off focus or shut it completely down. It may occur in a sentence, a mouthy comment, or through an unwillingness to follow the agenda of the class. They must be dealt with or your class will disintegrate. Here are some common Lesson Wreckers.

• *The diverters.* These kids ask question intended to get us off the topic. Usually they hit you in a favorite area, feigning interest in something that interests you. And off you go!

• *The "angelic" whammy.* During a retreat studying sex, a high school student asked the leader a simple but blunt question with the straightest face and looking like a cherub. The rest of the group lost it, laughing hysterically. However, as the teenager kept his face composed, the leader believed he was sincere and calmed the group down to answer the question. The rest of the intended discussion never happened.

• *The negative remark.* Cutting, biting, sarcastic remarks have a way of preventing our teaching because they get the rest of the kids to join in and cut up, too. A negative remark can completely neutralize what you are attempting to teach both by the words and the impact on spiritual truth.

• *The class clown.* Every class gets at least one. The joker who won't take anything seriously and draws sincere learners away with her or his wit.

• *Latecomers.* When someone comes in late, we often feel we must bring them up to the point in the lesson that the rest of the class holds, so we review for them, wasting class time and momentum.

• **Bad combinations.** Sometimes a group of great learners can be decimated by two or three who do not mix well when sitting together. They may argue, or joke, or just not focus on the instructions.

• **The authority challenger.** This wrecker questions you at every turn, trying to demean you before the rest of the class while elevating their own stature.

There are many more Lesson Wreckers, but you get the idea. To be successful in your teaching ministry, formulate strategies which can deal with these problems. Sometimes a person-to-person talk will suffice. Sometimes a call to the parents is necessary. Whatever it takes, as leader you have to take control and move the class away from the distraction.

These critical elements of teaching will help you to communicate the gospel of Jesus Christ to the students God has given you. Be imaginative in your delivery, creative in your preparation, and keep those eyes on Jesus.

One more thing, never underestimate the power of prayer. Prayer for your class, the students, the lessons, that God prepare their hearts to receive is not an option. It is part of our spiritual requirements. It is *the* element of your teaching that can change every other aspect of the time you invest in these lives.

8 *Learning Styles in the Classroom*

Oh for the good old days, when a student was only a student and teaching was simple and uneventful. Now, research, followed by a deluge of information on the varying styles of learning represented in an average classroom, has inundated us.

Ever hear about Einstein flunking math in high school? It is a true story and one wonders how the greatest mathematical genius of our time could do so poorly in a math class. Certainly it wasn't based on intelligence or ability, as he proved in his adult years. More likely it was a difference in his own personal learning style and the teaching approach of the teacher.

We have seen it time and again with our own children and the kids we work with at church. Barring personal family difficulties like a move, a job change, a death or a divorce which always puts a glitch in a student's academic performance, the most common learning problem is found in differences between a student's best learning avenue and the teacher's manner of teaching.

This chapter is meant to encourage us in our teaching abilities. Each of us wants to be the best communicator for Christ that we can be, and we all know that we can learn better skills and approaches to enhance classroom learning.

We will not make excuses for students with poor behavior or those who do not pay attention in class. Our society is already filled with every possible excuse for unacceptable growth and development. We must believe that anyone can learn on some level. Even those with learning disabilities can be excellent students. Beyond all our educational philosophies and strategies, we have the Lord Jesus Christ. "If God be for us, who can be against us?" (Romans 8:31).

This chapter turns our attention to two important considerations which will be evident in every classroom, sacred and secular. God created each of us to be a different and special miracle, so it is no surprise that we have many different kinds of teenagers in our high school classes. By this age, the learning styles are hardened cement. Any differences and difficulties are well seasoned and a part of who they are. By and large, the students are aware of their likes and dislikes; they are beginning to formulate an understanding of who they will become. Career plans are being considered and made. Colleges are being selected and visited.

However, there is much that they can still learn about their faith.

How We Learn - And Why We Don't

Recent studies and educational theories show that human intelligence is not the single factored logic based entity we thought it to be. In fact, some theorize that humans display seven or eight different types of intelligence, which may explain much of what we, as teachers and youth leaders, observe among our kids. For instance...

Bill was kind of a clumsy, dorky kid who, at first glance, had very little going for him. He had lots of difficulty in school, exhibiting a number of learning disabilities. Public school was a dead end for him. His parents placed him in a school for learning challenged kids that sought to teach using approaches not found in public school. Bill did better, but he still was below average in his accomplishments. Then he discovered music, and life has not been the same.

Bill is an extremely gifted musician, well above average in his ability to learn musically and very disciplined. He is gaining recognition among his peers for the first time in his life. Surprisingly, his clumsiness and dorky behavior have fallen aside, and an intelligent, wonderful teenager has emerged. The showy exterior is no longer needed. Bill has found God's gifts in his life.

Bill is a true example of how other kinds of differences, when discovered and groomed, can transform a young person into the person God intended them to be.

How come Johnny, who is flunking math and science, can learn a foreign language in no time? Why is it that Diane, who is so good in Bible history, can't pass her psychology class and has never learned to play an instrument? And Don, the captain of almost every sport in school, struggles with pencil and paper subjects but always excels in classes that allow him to use his hands or body to perform, such as shop, mechanics, and operating the sound board for his church's worship services?

It's because "book and paper" learning is only one way to educate our children. Learning in your classroom needs to accommodate many learning needs. This is true in public schools and in Sunday Schools.

Other means, which incorporate traditional methods of education with other equally important and successful approaches, may insure that each teenager has the opportunity to learn on many levels. This tends to be the kind of spiritual education that occurs on a retreat or at church camp. Why not make it a part of our classrooms or youth meetings?

Retreats usually incorporate plenty of Bible study time, perhaps some journaling or quiet study, lots of music and games, small and large group discussions, prayer, talk at the tables during meals, and all the rest. At retreats, we use many varied approaches to communicating the life-giving message of Jesus Christ. Thinking and talking, body motion in games, study time and applying what is learned, music, and so on. It seems we already know how to use different learning channels. But for some reason, we let those wait outside the Sunday School classroom.

Let's look at the ways in which we learn with some suggestions on practical application in teaching situations.

How We Learn

You have probably seen material on learning differences in the news or on a TV special. In general, there are four styles:

• *Relational/Innovative* learners want to talk about the lessons and relate on a "heart" or emotional level.

• *Analytical learners* want the facts and the opportunity to study and analyze them.

• *Commonsense/Kinesthetic* learners are "hands-on" types who enjoy independent projects.

• *Dynamic* learners thrive on activity and enjoy being in charge of something. Almost all students learn more by being involved and doing something than from just hearing it.

However, for kids of all ages and adults, the best learning occurs when the eye gate (visual learning) is integrated at all practical opportunities with auditory and hands-on experiences.

The fact is that our physical five senses, while universally used by most people, are not used equally by us as individuals. Each of us has a unique combination of how we channel our world to the thinking part of our brain. We see, smell, hear, taste and touch the world around us, and by these means we communicate to our brain what we experience in the world. Our brain blends these discoveries into our understanding of life. Our senses are our doorways to perception and learning.

However, when working with any group of two or more, the leader must be aware of how differences affect learning.

Some of us cannot resist a great hymn sing or a choir performance. Each word spoken in a sermon or Bible study brings meaning and relevancy to our lives. We like the radio programs our Christian stations offer. Life is experienced through our ears. We are **auditory** learners.

Others of us perceive life and the world around us listen, but we also see the passion of the preacher or choir. We watch faces, body language, the surroundings. We find great interest in charts, maps, drawings, and the like. Life comes to us through our eyes. We are **visual** learners.

Then some must hold a piece of pottery, play a game, get our hands into the paints to experience our world. We are **kinesthetic** learners who internalize by touching and being physically involved in the learning process. Holding a pottery shard from the Holy Land, we feel the excitement and a connection with how folks lived in Christ's time. A hug communicates more than a handshake. Any hands-on learning activities teaches us more about life than any other way.

One style is not better than another. Many people blend these styles into different combinations and in different situations. These are simply different ways in which different people best connect with and relate to their world. Incorporating all of these types of styles will benefit every study in your youth group.

Each of these channels also blends with individual learning styles. A learning style is expressed through the way we best enjoy learning what our personal learning channel brings to us.

Let's look at the four styles through the example of a youth talk challenging high schoolers with relationship evangelism.

• **Relational/Innovative** learners interact with what they are learning through talking about the "heart" of the lesson. They are attracted to the emotional level of the topic and strongly desire to understand truth by what they are feeling. Talking about the love of Jesus for the lost sparks in them a need to share with those who do not know Jesus or the great love He has for them. In their hearts they can feel the alienation and loneliness of those who do not know Christ.

• **Analytical learners** want facts, facts, facts! They love to study and research. In their homes you'll find their personal copies of various study guides and maybe a research book or two. These kids continually borrow our Bible on CD-ROM to use at home. Analysis of the subject is a great joy to these learners. As you share your message on evangelism, they are thinking about the various verses that can be used and how the New Testament church related to the lost the message of Christ's love.

• **Commonsense/Kinesthetic** learners enjoy independent projects, especially a "hands-on" project which can be built or developed to support the lesson. Give them the job of witnessing for Christ by planning a work camp to a needy part of your town. They'll also want to have a cook out for the whole group, workers and recipients, at the end of the project so they can cook the burgers.

• **Dynamic** learners love projects which allow them to lead in some capacity or which put them in charge of an aspect of the lesson. They need to help you if a program is developed for taking the group to a weekend training retreat. Putting them in charge of food lists, room assignments, and announcements makes them feel that they are helping in the learning for all.

Of course, after you find your own personal learning style, you'll likely note that the others also have some level of familiarity. Fact is, all of us are probably best described as having a mixture of the four with a dominant style. In terms of high schoolers, it is a fact of youth work that teenagers learn more by being involved using their governing style than from just hearing about sharing their faith.

The differing styles do not have to be a problem. The key is to convert each lesson into a multi-leveled experience which at least touches upon the styles of every learner. Of course, some lessons adapt better than others. And some seem nearly impossible to augment. The chapter on adapting a topic will give you ideas and suggestions.

One of the simplest ways to reach each of the the learning avenues and insure understanding is to develop a vocabulary that reflects visual, auditory, dynamic, and kinesthetic words. This is an incredibly powerful tool for effectively sharing the gospel with any group. Jesus used this tool in

His own ministry. Read the Sermon on the Mount or His parables and begin listing the kinds of words He uses to describe His messages. Note how many words are used in each mode.

When sharing a youth talk with high schoolers, or even when preaching in the services of our church, Mark works to describe his illustrations with multi-level wording. In describing a setting, like a gathering on Memorial Day in our town square, he might describe the colors of the day or the uniforms of the musicians or military color guard. He might also note that it was a cool and breezy morning, with a hint of moisture in the air and talk about how the emotions of the crowd were so thick you could feel the respect for those who died serving our country.

Then, to relate to the auditory learner, he might describe the music or voices of the school choir, play a portion of the music, and make reference to the speech remarking on some quotes.

Each of these can be accomplished within any lesson by adding only a couple of sentences from time to time to enhance the lesson on each level. It is not difficult, but it takes some time and effort in the beginning to gather a repertoire of descriptive words.

Unfortunately, there are still too few books within the Christian world on these concerns. An excellent resource is *Learning Styles: Reaching Everyone God Gave You To Teach,* by Marlene LeFever.

If our goal is to honor all of the learning styles that God gifted us with, then we need to be proactive in our lesson preparation and in leading our youth programs.

How well do you know your students? Make a list this week and try to identify which is their best learning style and in what combinations do they operate? Test yourself and know how best to present Jesus Christ to each student. You—and they—will be eternally glad you did.

9 *Differences and Learning*

We know a teen who has horrible eyesight. His corrective lenses do not fully correct his vision problems. His thick glasses reduce all he sees to about one-third less the size of what it really is. His view of life is similar to that of seeing our world through a rear view, passenger side car mirror. He is a bright kid.

However, until a Sunday School teacher began enlarging his Sunday School work, he seemed disinterested and unimpressed by the things of God. Once his lessons were enlarged so he could see them better, he developed a keen interest in Sunday School. His mother even commented that it was no longer a chore to get him up on Sunday morning. His limitations were obstacles. Once solved, he excelled.

Another teen we know has Attention Deficit Disorder (ADD) which is characterized by such symptoms as being unable to pay attention, troubles in organizing, acting out impulsively, and being restless or hyperactive. His self-esteem was low, and he had no confidence, having come to expect rejection and ridicule.

This teenager was diagnosed in his late junior high years and has received a some extra support from understanding church leaders. Again, we have witnessed an almost miraculous change in interest and behavior.

Currently, he is his school's class president and an innovative, creative thinker for school programs. He is also a leader in youth group and continually offers input to the advisors as to how they can better help kids like him. He knows when another teen like him is in class and is a wonder with them, making them feel comfortable.

The same story came our way with another young woman. She found Sunday School, youth group, Girl Scouts, and public school to be extremely difficult and received little gratification in her life. Life turned around for her when her parents discovered a school especially designed for learning disabled kids. Erica found her grades rising, her self-esteem being repaired, and her outlook on life improving. And suddenly, Sunday School and other youth programs were great. She told me once that learning disabilities are often learning differences. Differences is a much easier word to live with.

Learning disabilities—or differences—are common in our teenagers.

As teachers of teens, if we become aware of the varieties of differences that we may find among our students and learn some basic approaches to help them learn, we will give the kids further proof that the risen Savior created them and accepts them for who they are, as they are, with the promise of a life of fulfillment in Him.

Learning disabilities are often affiliated with problems in the central nervous system. Sometimes the nervous system throws obstacles in the ways we learn. Learning functions get interrupted, interfered with, or upset, and the student finds it next to impossible to take in or process what is being offered in class. When the more common distractions of the teenage years are added, troubles like daydreaming, worries, fatigue, depression, or problems at home, then learning and participation in class may be all but impossible.

Four quadrants of dealing with information are generally affected by learning disabilities. As a teacher, knowing these may help you determine which area of information processing is difficult for the teenager. If you know, you will have an easier time understanding, leading, and guiding these teens in your programs. To become knowledge, a lesson has to travel through the normal treatment each of these four quadrants imposes to become part of our repertoire of comprehension.

First, we have to accurately **collect the information**. Problems in collection may be seen in the inability to differentiate between distance, size, amount, or the wording of what is being taught. These variables are incorrectly noted, and the collection of the data is inaccurate. For example, the student may hear you say Jesus fed the 4,000 but collect it as Jesus fed 40. So what's the big deal? Their grandma feeds 40 every Thanksgiving.

After information is collected, the brain will **sort the information** into ways it can be held in the mind as knowledge. If the student cannot properly sort the data correctly, distortions may arise. Often, matching difficulties or problems in seeing small details are overlooked in sorting. Here, when studying the missionary journeys in the book of Acts, the student may continually mix up the cities visited by Paul and completely miss large areas of his journeys.

How the brain **stores the information** may also be interfered with. Memory is often poor and the order of a lesson may be distorted or mixed up. Memorizing the books of the Bible is nearly impossible for these students, as is matching of sounds, sentences, or even concepts with a number of steps or points.

Finally, some will be unable to **express the information** which has been learned. They cannot say back what they know. Sometimes speech is affected, or it cannot be written, or, if expressed in motion, cannot be duplicated in order or accuracy.

By the high school years teens with learning disabilities of one kind or another have often learned ways to avoid the embarrassment or frustration of the disability by avoiding or compensating for the barrier.

We work with kids who are often ridiculed or seem to be friendless due to these problems. Perhaps you can bring to mind an active and interested high schooler who participates in regular meetings of youth group but often avoids Sunday School. The student may be trying to bypass the "book learning" which is next to impossible for her or him. Since learning disabilities have no real noticeable physical clues or cues, we may assume that the teenager is less devoted to the things of God than they actually are. To their thinking, why face the frustration or embarrassment?

As leaders and teachers, the challenge becomes one of how we can help them learn to learn. Many learning disabilities go unnoticed and untreated. In your classroom you can expect that up to a third of the kids you teach have some form of learning disabilities.

But, it is never too late to help.

Learning problems make the student feel immensely frustrated or even stupid. It damages their view of themselves as competent people. They find that avoidance is a better, more reliable solution than any other form of treatment. We might want to learn what we can do to help them so that their knowledge of salvation, commitment, and service is not sidetracked.

The right environment is thought to be one of the greatest benefits to those with learning barriers. Learning challenged teenagers will respond to your understanding of their troubles. You can increase their participation through such considerations as giving them some special attention or assigning an adult advisor to work with them. Often a smaller group experience works better for them than the large group lectures. Keeping a regular schedule that they are aware of before any meeting or event is a great confidence builder. However, they may need some additional encouragement from you.

There are some common challenges to learning which are likely to be seen in your classroom.

• Attention Deficit Disorder (ADD) and Attention Deficit Hyperactive Disorder (ADHD) are two learning barriers which are evidenced by such behaviors as restlessness, squirming, being easily distracted, talking loudly or out of turn, problems in understanding instructions, uncompleted tasks, and interruptions.

• Dyslexia includes reading based difficulties in which words or letters appear inverted or backwards causing confusion and learning barriers, and writing based difficulties in which the student may have trouble forming letters as they are seen. Some may write backwards.

• Some students are unable to understand how numbers work. They cannot order numerically or work numbers for solutions.

• Some have trouble hearing and speaking. They mix up the order of words in a sentence or are unable to process instructions as they are heard. Repeating as heard may be impossible.

• Attention spans vary in length and development. We often read of generalized attention spans and attempt to conduct our classes accordingly. However, some students will only be able to sit a quarter or a third of the standard time which most teenagers can remain quiet or focused.

• Also common are problems with poor impulse control, anger, frustration, and appropriate behavior. When these young adults reach their limits of personal control, they may become disruptive, squirmy, or lose attention.

• Some physical problems may be a hindrance to learning and worth your consideration. Hearing loss problems, problems of coordination or low motor abilities, eye problems, or speech limitations may prevent their participation or limit what they experience in learning.

Some learning styles may be developed as a compensation to learning disabilities. We know a number of teenagers with very poor eyesight who have learned to take in information through auditory channels, thus limiting the problems of reading or seeing, or by kinesthetic means, which enables them to manipulate the lesson through touching.

Symptoms for discerning learning problems come in two categories which, when learned and looked for, can be very helpful in determining if a student has some disabilities.

Physical signs include slow speech or speech that is hard to understand. A teenager may be overactive to the point of disruption. Sometimes bad coordination is a good indicator of learning barriers.

Behavioral signs can be a clue, too. At times every teenager cuts up or acts inappropriately. But if these problems continue and behavior is not moderated through a warning or a request to settle down, take note. If a teenager exhibits lots of anger, long-term moodiness, an inability to concentrate, an unusually short attention span, or low control over impulses, she or he may be learning disabled and will need you to make proper concessions for them. Also be on the look out for trouble in organizing thoughts, restlessness, distractibility, poor memory, and a drop off in attendance. The first step to helping is to begin to know what they face.

You can compensate for each of these learning challenges in the classroom using the follow approaches.

1. If you are entering a new classroom situation, be it Sunday School or youth group, contact the parents of your students and ask them about any learning problems their teenagers may have. This knowledge is a powerful tool in understanding each student and giving them the proper treatment and attention they need in order to learn.

2. Spend some time in the library or with one of the many books on disabilities and make a laundry list of learning differences with their identifying characteristics. Then learn the particulars of the problems included in your classroom. Many of them sound huge and threatening at first, but they crumble like Goliath before young David's sling when you find out what is actually involved. You may also become more alert to problem situations and be able to see learning disabilities of which both parents and students may be unaware.

3. Browse your curriculum with an open mind. Consider how to adapt it appropriately with extra

steps and minor changes to insure that each student may benefit from the lesson. A curriculum publisher must publish to a generic audience. It is up to the teacher to know the students well enough to adapt it for any specific learning difficulties. A lesson must touch lives or it is not a lesson worth our time. Small changes may make it appropriate to every student in the class.

4. Keep in mind that these are high school students whose learning styles and disabilities are fairly well established. This does not mean they will never change or benefit from your effort. It may mean that they are not accustomed to being able to learn, or to having a teacher work to insure their success. Some teenagers will react with anger or become offended if they are made aware of what you are doing. Teachers in their past experiences may not have tried to help them. Make your teaching effort seamless so no one in the class is made to stand out. They may feel they are being "babied" to learn. It is better to make your changes for everyone so that the students with the problems might benefit.

Remember that teenagers of normal to high intelligence may still find learning a problem. It is not based on how bright one is, but on how information is gathered and processed. When failure has become a way of life, it is hard to envision it any differently.

We opened the previous chapter lamenting the "good old days" when we all were treated the same in our classes, both secular and church based. It was so much easier not to know what we know these days.

However, we have a better chance to serve our students and our God through the greater information within our grasp. As stewards of God, we need to consider this data and use it in our Sunday Schools so that each teen gets just what is needed. Our calling as teachers and leaders requires us to be the very best communicator of God we can be. The rewards may sometimes seem long in coming. But when a life is changed for God, our Bible says there is joy in Heaven over one sinner who repents (Luke 15:7).

Some kids with learning problems may never hear that message clearly unless you make the extra effort to know and understand.

10 Relevancy and Learning Styles

Of all the possible questions potential leaders or teachers may ask, the ones we often listen for are those which openly and honestly question her or his personal ability to be relevant to high school age teenagers. To make a difference. To be the kind of leader that a teenager can connect with. If the teacher candidate is concerned about this factor, and is willing to listen and learn, we know that we are talking to a good candidate.

Relevancy is the best key we know of in teaching and guiding high schoolers into a lifelong faith in Jesus Christ. Jesus came as one of us. He experienced life as we experience it. He knows what it was, and is, like to be human in a lost and hurting world (Hebrews 4:14-16). In that we find confidence to trust him as Lord.

Teenagers wonder the same about us. How often do we hear, "You just don't understand!" This cry comes from the heart of today's youth. They need us to reassure them that we were teenagers once (and don't they just love to tease us on how long ago that was!), and that we haven't forgotten what it was like to have a first kiss or to be tempted to cheat on a test. This is the nitty-gritty of their lives. How they negotiate these issues, and many others, will determine their ability to meet the rest of life hand-in-hand with the Savior. If they believe that you can help because you understand, then they will accept you as their teacher.

To be relevant, you have to practice empathy, or putting on the shoes of the other person to see what life is like for him or her. This is something Jesus exhibited continually in His ministry and which Christians have practiced for years. We call it compassion—the ability to feel the other person's pain, joy, troubles, victories, and all the other emotions of life. Relevancy demands that you open your heart and love them without any restrictions or conditions. It also insists that you lead or teach by "speaking the truth in love" for to be relevant does not mean we give up what we know is right in Christ. We listen, we reflect, we share, we teach—but we use God's Word as our ultimate guide. Relevancy is not blind acceptance or carte blanche approval. It is offering support and guidance for the high schoolers in this particular time of their lives.

What is Relevant to High Schoolers?

We do forget. We were young once, but not yesterday. Reviewing what is relevant to teen-agers today by looking back and remembering how it was in our lives will only get us so far. We have to pay attention to what the kids are teaching us about their world today, both verbally and non-verbally.

Ask them to tell you what it's like these days. They will be their own best spokespersons and, as they trust you, they'll keep you posted. Read the magazines they read. Catch some of their programs on TV or listen to some of their favorite music artists. You may be somewhat shocked and even offended—but this is the world in which they live. Know the faith conflicts they face from their real-world perspective.

Remaining relevant is remaining informed. Giving relevant lessons is a matter of taking what you learn and mixing it into the lessons being taught in a form they will accept and respond to. There are no short cuts.

As teachers, we need to remind ourselves that consistent relevancy in our teaching occurs when we open our classrooms in welcome to all styles of learning, as well as the topics which kids find important. Yet, if an important topic misses their best avenue of learning, they will become disinterested.

Here is a sample of how a lesson can be made relevant and interesting to the young people in your class.

Facing Your Goliath

Although it is a commonly known Bible story, the account of David's meeting and defeating of Goliath is almost in the "legend" category to our young people, not because it is unbelievable, but because they have heard it a zillion times. The story has little application to their lives because it is so well known. The same is true with other stories like Daniel and the Lion's Den or Jesus changing water to wine. Having heard them so many times, many students will not automatically import the application into their own lives. High schoolers may need some help finding meaningful and fitting applications of the value of the story to their own experience.

Programming with relevance means you seek new ways to interpret the Bible events for the youth in your church. It means providing pertinent applications from their day-to-day lives using what is troubling them as the Goliath to be defeated. Often we default to just laying the application out for them. However, this breaks a cardinal rule of learning—we own what we have invested in.

You do not have to relegate such Bible events to the elementary grades. Approach these lessons with each type of learner in mind, yet without presuming upon Scripture or trying to import feelings not present in God's account.

To grab the attention of the **Imaginative learner**, describe the feelings of the characters. David's confidence in God could be described as stronger than any fear generated by the challenge of the enormous man before him. He faced the situation, trusted God, and let the stones sail. *People* are important to imaginative learners, as are discussions and ideas. These learners can be hooked by role playing the dilemma of the confrontation. They can easily name the Goliaths in their lives with some coaching, or through your opening up and describing your personal and challenging Goliaths. They turn off to lectures analyzing the account or having to work on the story alone with pencil and paper approaches.

For these learners, you might develop a Goliath Project to study this event. After reading the story to the group, introduce a project which will illustrate this story. It is called the Goliath Project. In the Goliath Project, you might create a physical game, using homemade sling shots and pebbles. Each student can make a Goliath shape from cardboard. Depending on time limitations, they can decorate the Goliath. Attached to the front of each giant could be a business envelop into which each student can put their Goliaths—the problems or people which confound them, trouble them, steal their hope. Then, play the game of seeing who can knock their Goliath over first, or who can hit it the most times with their rocks, or in a time allowance. Even though fun, the activity demonstrates David actually had to work to slay his foe.

To conclude, re-read the story as a group and remark that our Goliaths do not just disappear, they require effort and preparation to overcome them. Most importantly, they require our faith and confidence in God and our willingness to stand for Him in every situation no matter how potentially fearful or intimidating. Encourage them to pray about the Goliaths in their envelopes. Make sure they take the envelopes with them at the end of the meeting. Insuring their privacy is important.

Adapting this lesson for the **Analytic learner** would address their needs for information to be presented in order with a logical, examinable beginning and ending. These learners love facts and tend to see life in blacks and whites with the emphasis on the correct. You might see these learners jotting in their Bibles as the story is being read. This story is great for them because they love seeing winners and losers. For the Goliath Project to be fun for them, it has to have some time for them to work alone. They may need help in translating their difficulties to something as abstract as a cardboard figure with an envelop attached that is to hold their shortcomings or sins. Yet, if you make the principles of the story plain, they will participate and learn.

Common Sense learners will need the Goliath Project to have a clear goal with some practical lesson and vital moral. They like to learn in the midst of noise, and they thrive on projects which allow movement or hands on involvement. These are action people who like to work out the solutions to a difficulty on their own. You can direct, but do not do it for them. If the Goliath can be built with some flair, they will rise to the challenge. That there is some action in the activity will hook them. Knowing that the Goliath Project may offer them some workable information in solving their personal difficulties will make it all worth it.

Dynamic learners will value the Goliath Project for its dramatic, artsy quality. Movement and some creativity will gain their attention. Dynamic learners like to experiment with new ideas and need some flexible ways to learn. If it is an unusual means of teaching, they want to try it. Being intuitive, they can make good decisions. Liking people and group projects, they will thrive on seeing the rest of the group in their work. The meaning of the Goliath Project will not be lost on them.

In a project like this, we deal with each learner's needs and avenues of accepting information. We communicate a life-giving story with meaning that is relevant to today's teenage world. We provide hope in the example of David while diminishing the feared giants which hold us back from serving God as fully as we could. We create an educational experience that is hands-on, different, memorable, and non-typical. It is the kind of lesson that will remain with them and one that they will likely reminisce upon in future gatherings with those immortal, "Do you remember the time we..." words.

So What's A Teacher To Do?

You have all of the necessary material and information available to conduct a legendary youth program in your church. Let's look at another concrete example of how a lesson can be made more relevant to our youth.

The "Game of Life" Income Event

Jesus told us that the poor and needy will be with us always. Further, the Bible has hundreds of verses which tell us to help the needy, the orphan, the widow. These are the less fortunate, the destitute. Jesus asks us to reach out to them by offering help in His name. The principle in Matthew 25:31-46 clearly extends our ministry to the hungry, those in jail, and those who are ill.

We have offered a special youth group meeting at which the kids are divided up through a number of information clues that designate for them their income level, their expenses, their health, their level of faith, their occupation, and their disposable income. Then the kids are assigned a number of issues to face, basing their decisions on their life situations.

Two kids receive an income of $10,000 per month; a few draw $5,000 or $3,000 per month; others receive $1,000, $500, and finally welfare of $262.00 per month with food coupons. Then the occupations are drawn, the number of children they have, if they are married, divorced, the level of their health, and the rest. The kids draw a slip from each stack and the accumulation is their "life." We get them to talk about their lives, describing how it feels to be the person they have invented.

Once they are well into the role, we ask them to pick a dilemma sheet to discover what is going on in their lives. They have to apply the life they invented to some real life problems, such as: A child is diagnosed with cancer; you've just lost your job, or your church is entering a building project and has asked for your help. Again, they must think it through, report how life is in this situation, and why they make the decisions they do.

This event takes work and preparation. However, it is a life changer. It involves every learning style, addresses a number of major issues of concern to the kids, teaches them about responsibility, helps them step into the world of adult living, and puts before them the uncertainty of life. The kids who are "issued" a personal relationship with Christ get to explain how we can lean on Him. The kids without Christ have to trudge on without hope.

Events like this also appeal to the needs of some to lead, of others to plan, and the like. A major event like this cannot happen without planning and cooperation. Even the kids who help plan can still participate. It works especially well at a weekend retreat.

We finish this event with a debriefing time of open discussion and a devotion focusing in on Christ's love and care for us in the midst of our varied and often complicated lives.

Scripture assures us that we may cast "all your care upon him; for he careth for you" (I Peter 5:7). This event brings the reality of Jesus to the problem and creates the kind of experience that makes numerous Bible verses more real to all of us—student and teacher alike. It assures us that God is concerned about each bird in the air, the hairs on our heads, clothing the flowers of the field.

These are the kinds of events that the kids thrive on. There is action, motion, some freedom through random choices, and it places them in a life they have not yet lived. Plus, the event teaches them Christian values from a biblical perspective.

Using your imagination, you can alter and adapt such an event to be quite personal for your program.

11 *Adapting a Topic*

It was during Mark's first summer as a minister to youth while at church camp with 27 vibrant teenagers that he learned a secret to reaching kids: they love it when you do the spontaneous and unexpected.

It was through observing an older minister that he realized how one could adapt a topic in ways that extended the topic's relevancy with the setting in mind. Pastor Gene did not abandon what had been selected for the lesson; he simply "tweaked" it a bit to grab the kids. It's an effective method for youth ministry.

The setting was a beautiful central Ohio campground on a brilliant July afternoon. It was Bible study time, and we were studying Christ's parables. The lesson was great, however, it had been designed for a classroom setting. It needed some adaptation to offer it to kids sitting in the midst of God's fabulous creation.

Pastor Gene, sensing the kids' inattentiveness, closed the leader's guide and said, "I need some volunteers so we can look at this lesson differently."

He had their attention, but, at first, no one volunteered. Then, one brave hand shot up. Pastor Gene invited the teenager up front. With the ice broken, about half of the group volunteered for the yet unknown project.

Next, Pastor Gene asked Mark to get his guitar and to play some slow, easy music. Then he gave assignments to the volunteers. Using the Parable of the Sower, he assigned kids to be the various seed, the weeds, the birds, the sower, and so on. Then, without any rehearsal, he announced to the rest of the group that we would "see" a reading of the Parable of the Sower.

As Mark played his guitar, Pastor Gene slowly read the parable, watching as the volunteers interpreted it. Then, we did it again. And a third time.

Each presentation was more polished. The "actors" had time to try new expressions. Mark tried various lines of music and attempted to catch the mood of the sentence being played out.

The proof of the exercise was evident as Pastor Gene then reopened his leader's guide and used the rest of the lesson to discuss the parable. With a strong grasp on the parable, the entire group discussed its meaning and how to apply it to their own lives enthusiastically.

Pastor Gene intuitively sought to communicate the lesson on all of the learning style levels. The music and slow reading reached the auditory learners. The acting was good for the kinesthetic learners. The chance to move around helped the kids with attention span challenges. Visual learners "saw" the story. Plus, and this is important to high schoolers, it seemed as though we were "breaking the rules" by setting the leader's guide aside for a few moments.

We, as teachers, must be sensitive to the group dynamics present. We must mold a lesson to the special dynamics and qualities of our specific situations.

The application of any lesson to your class is your responsibility. The teacher alone can take the material, see the lesson truths and application, then adapt the topic to fit the kinds of teenagers gathered in your class.

Sometime ago Mark had an especially artistically talented group in his Sunday School class. The Christian Education Supervisor had selected a great study with lots of relevant material for the teenagers. Yet, it fell short week after week. Mark fretted quite a bit over the problem. Was it the kids? Were the lessons outdated? Did the book use language the kids couldn't understand? Did we have a classroom of learning challenged students? To each question the answer was "no." In every regard, the classes should be successful. But they weren't.

Kathy noted that the kids were artistic and supplied some suggestions for artistic adaptation of the lessons. Not being artistic, Mark tried to decline. But she prevailed, and the class was transformed. The kids responded to the various truths of the lessons by working with them in projects. We made posters. We tore pictures from magazines and made a group collage. Some drawings were produced. And, although not carried out, we discussed how a mural could be developed from the whole series. Their creative sparks were flying and suddenly the kids loved Sunday School.

Various Methods of Lesson Adaptation

Curriculum is a wonderful tool. In it you have the experience of professional educators to lead you through specified topics. Their gift to the body of Christ is their research and preparation of a biblically sound and potentially life-changing set of lessons for you to share with your class in a consistent coverage of the Bible. Your gift is to apply these "black on white" words into life-changing lessons that the teenagers will internalize.

Let's look at some means by which we may adapt any lesson to met the specific or special needs of our classrooms. We assume you have a good knowledge of your kids—their limitations, their strengths, their interests, their fears, their priorities. Now, imagine how it might work if you used some of the following.

Music. Can the current lesson be strengthened by some well known chorus? Or by handing out the words from a hymn and singing it at appropriate places during the lesson discussion? Perhaps a contemporary tune draws from the Scripture used in the lesson. When inserted as a reinforcement, music can be a wonderful addition to most any topic.

Or...allow the kids to divide in groups of about five and write songs using some standard tune. The assignment might be to create a song which tells the story of the Prodigal Son using the tune to "Mary Had a Little Lamb." Then, the creating group has to sing it to the other groups.

While laughter is certain to accompany the outcome, that will enhance the classroom atmosphere.

The kids will examine the depth of God's love and acceptance for us, as well as the need to turn away from aimlessness and sin, as they study the Scripture passage to write the words. The lesson is not made less serious. It is just experienced differently.

Music is **the** way many kids relate to their world and culture today, even more than through visual imagery. A popular song will influence their clothing, set apart social groups, define a school year, or identify an illusive feeling or belief. Be careful not to trash their songs or music. An outright attack will erode your relationship with them. It is far better to offer a short explanation on why a song is in error or inappropriate. Compare the lyrics with a particular passage of Scripture and let the kids decide what's wrong. Build bridges, not barriers.

Current songs, both secular and sacred, can be used to evaluate the issues which kids want to discuss or consider. Use a song as a springboard to examine the Bible's position on the issue comparatively. Suddenly, the song becomes a teaching and learning tool, linking God's Word to their lives and fostering serious consideration of just what they are listening to and how it affects them.

Mark annually holds a music night for the youth and allows them to bring in any song they wish, secular or sacred. They have to identify the theme of the song, tell why they like it, and the message it offers. We admit, some of the songs have been shocking! Yet, in allowing this exercise, we have opened up many avenues which bring Christ and their faith to a "hands on" clarifying filter of their culture. We are not critics; they are the analysts. In listening to the music and making them be responsible for the explanation, they apply Christ's standards as a relevant part of life. Godly seeds are planted as they are encouraged to wrestle through the unhealthy and dangerous messages found in some of today's music.

Drama. Spontaneous drama can demonstrate the lesson being studied. Other ways to use drama might include assigning the writing and performing of skits or short, one act plays to re-enact a lesson. Mark has done this by giving the kids assigned character, setting, and dilemma "facts" on 3 x 5 cards and allowing them to develop their own scripts. They assign the characters and enact the dilemma within the assigned setting.

In doing this, you can change details of familiar Bible stories or lessons to allow the kids a personal experience with the story. Adapt the missionary experiences of Paul in the context of today's current events and situations. Or, act out Christ's last week but change the primary role throughout the week to one of the disciples or Mary and let them tell what they see and feel. If you select Peter walking on water, ask them to identify what makes them take their eyes off Jesus, select one to portray, and show how to stay focused on God rather than our circumstances.

Drama is a great tool because it allows us to step out of our lives and try something else. We all learn through playing the part of someone else because we must "get into" the role and understand that character's motivation. Our teenagers can have the same experiences as they portray biblical events or characters and discover that these "stories" are the record of real people, just like them.

Art. Many of us, as leaders and teachers, find art intimidating. Rather than shy away from an artistic lesson application, trust the kids to take the project seriously and watch with amazement the results they produce. Kids seem to be attracted to art in ways that most "non-artsie" adults find unbelievable. *Kids love avenues of self-expression which produce a product at the end.* Art is a valuable way to achieve this goal.

Creative artistic expression goes way beyond coloring or finger painting. One church allowed young people the use of a very large, very public wall to develop a mural showing a peaceful scene. Nearly twenty years later it is still intact. The teenagers rose to the occasion and went well beyond expectations.

Here are some ideas for employing art as a means to adapt a topic.

• Cut pictures from magazines to form a collage depicting a specific Scripture or a biblical concept. One high schooler cut out hundreds of small faces and glued them to posterboard in the shape of a pine tree around Christmas to underscore the meaning of Christmas—that Christ came for all.

• Let groups paint an ongoing scene on long rolls of paper that show modern application of some Bible truth in action over time, like the missionary journeys of Paul. Display these in prominent areas with short explanations.

• When studying the battle between sinful and godly living, let the kids illustrate their two, battling natures. A two-sided face divided by a line of two different colors of paper, coupled with collage pictures to show their inner struggles is one idea.

• "I Wonder" books take questions about faith and turn them into a project which illustrates the answers they discover through study. Again, they can draw or glue magazine images to pages to create their booklets.

• Illuminated lettering is an intricate art form similar to that used by the scribes in medieval days to begin a paragraph. Enclose the first letter of the first word in a square and then detail it with swirls or symbols. High schoolers can make wonderful illuminated letters for Bible verses which show what they have learned.

• Addressing issues or contemporary topics— you might require groups of two or three teenagers to develop some symbolic representation of the topic. For instance: *Friendship looks like…. Racism looks like…. Cheating on a school test makes me feel like….*

Guest speakers. Billing a special speaker as an expert is not as impressive to young adults as it may be to us. Better to advertise the speaker as exactly what she or he is. Forget the hype.

Kids respond well to speakers who are humorous, relevant, "one of them," or inspiring. They don't appreciate phonies or a speaker who comes off distant or insincere. However, bring in a speaker who can talk "to" kids, not "at" kids, and you will create a very successful learning atmosphere.

After bringing in numerous speakers to address the problems of drugs and alcohol for our youth group, with little success or impact, we finally decided to call our state highway patrol office to enlist the experiences of a patrolman. His talk was factual, honest, emotional, and seeded with many personal observations. Never did he tell the teenagers how to be or what to do. Rather, he let the volume of his encounters do the talking. The kids were affected dramatically.

Another wonderful use of speakers is to assemble a panel discussion about an issue. The lesson may include a discussion of Paul's "tent making" practice of working while he taught others about Christ. To accentuate this concept you might bring in five or six faithful church members to talk about how they relate their faith to their world while on the job. Nothing convinces young adults better than the testimony of those who have successfully integrated their faith to daily living. You can't argue with a testimony.

Object lessons. Any lesson can be helped with a relevant object lesson. Once while discussing the crucifixion with our church's youth, we prominently displayed a large, rough, wooden cross as we talked about what Jesus did for us through His sacrifice. Later, in youth group, we went through the horrible facts about death by crucifixion. The actual object made the lesson more meaningful.

Object lessons underline the words you say and make for "hands on" discussions or questions. Kathy has purchased fertilized eggs from farmers and incubated them until they hatched to demonstrate the new life we have through transformation in Jesus. The miracle of new life as seen in the baby chicks makes the words unforgettable.

Teenagers feel detached if we, as leaders, offer "adultized," lifeless, unimaginative lessons. We have heard high schoolers lament the fact that the church only offers "cool" lessons to the younger children. There is simply no reason not to offer appropriate object lessons to high schoolers.

Symbols. Our faith is rich with many symbols that express our recognition of Christ's work. The cross, a fish, a loaf of bread, water, and many more add to our understanding by providing the "eye gate" entrance to a recognizable reflection of the truth being learned.

The American flag stirs us as we stand at the beginning of a baseball game. The flag, with its colors of blue and red and white, is not our country. But we esteem it as our symbol. It inspires us. It motivates us. It reminds us of all that it stands for without lengthy lectures. It collects us together as a people.

The same is true with Christian symbols. Symbols which naturally tie into a lesson will underline the larger concepts we are teaching our high schoolers.

Symbols do not replace our beliefs. Rather, they allow us to identify with something greater than ourselves. For some, they will become the concrete representations of the lesson truths, as well as the time spent with you in the study.

Games. Even high schoolers love to think they are getting a classroom break by the insertion of a game. For instance, turn the answer of a question that has no quick respondent into a game of hangman. Drop from nowhere the declaration that, "Looks like we have to use hangman" and jot the number of lines in the single word answer on a chalkboard or on newsprint. Then, point and ask for a letter from the kids. This works best with words that have many letters.

After the brief game, return to the lesson without delay. The idea is not to detract from the lesson, but to insert an unexpected learning "break."

Don't use this frequently or the kids will withhold answers to get you to delay class. A spontaneous use once in awhile will maintain its learning advantages. You are seen as a teacher who is not overly serious, even when the topic is. High school kids love this quality in a leader.

The goal is to freshen the learning environment, not to detract from it with games.

Other Adaptation Ideas

Small group study and reports. Most of us use small groups and small group reports for study and discussion. Groups of eight or less do best, with twos and threes allowing for optimum exploration. Use small groups to keep the kids in touch with each other as they move through a lesson or to brainstorm together ways to resist temptation, make a difference as Christians, show their faith at school, respond to parents' rules, etc..

Anticipated Q and A. After browsing a lesson, Mark often plays with possible questions which may strengthen the message or goal. "What questions do I naturally ask myself after reading the verse or explanation?" Noting them may anticipate the questions of your students.

Incorporate your questions into the lesson and answer them. This technique displays your personal involvement with the issue, verse, or topic. It models for the teenagers the questioning mind we all naturally have from God. It gives them permission to ask deeper questions. The answers personalize the lesson. Never be afraid of hard questions. Plus, asking the questions yourself will help the shy, the visitor, or the "too cool to talk" to hear the answer to a question they may not be willing or able to ask.

Open discussion. Teenagers tend to do some of their best thinking when their mouths are moving. In terms of class management, this may be somewhat troubling. But in terms of learning or grasping a concept, it may be essential.

Some psychologists believe that we westerners do tend to speak before we think. It is not so much a problem as it is a style of processing our thoughts. For some of us, if we don't say it, we really don't have a chance to work with whatever it is we are thinking. This seems especially true for some teenagers.

This is somewhat risky because you never know what might be said. Yet, to not allow these kinds of discussions may mean that internal application of the material does not occur. If the kids are not thinking it, they will never live it.

Honest, open, no-holds-barred discussion is a valuable means by which our teenagers may learn spiritual truths. Christ asked mind boggling questions of His disciples such as, "Who do men say I am?" If the discussion reveals wrong thinking or non-Christian beliefs, then rejoice. You have an opportunity to "fine tune" what the student thinks with Scripture.

Jesus was not afraid to ask the questions, and He was not afraid of the answers as He allowed His disciples the freedom to grapple with hard issues. He did not look for automatic responses. Jesus wanted His followers' honest responses. Then He used those to correct or teach them God's truth.

As teachers, we should be confident enough to allow for a wrong answer. In challenging the students to think, we also need to provide them the space to not know or to make mistakes. An honest response that is incorrect can be changed by the high schooler as she or he thinks through the issue in the light of God's Word. Remember, the "paint" is still wet.

Most groups thrive on the discussion moment. It helps young believers understand that our faith grows over time. It is not something immediately understood or received intact at salvation. Be ready to shape the discussion with the Bible's answer, not just your own.

Question box. Years ago at church camp, we discovered that high schoolers have certain areas which they cannot comfortably discuss. Yet, they have innumerable questions. Such was the barrier in our annual sex talk.

To enable them to ask questions, we put out a "Sex Talk Question Box" and advertised among the kids that there were no questions that were off limits, and we would do our best to provide answers. Our disclaimer was that we, as counselors, would only respond with the Christian view of sex and that if we did not know, we would be honest and tell them.

Given the chance to ask with total anonymity, the "Sex Talk Question Box" was filled with more inquiries than time permitted for response. Of course, we received some rather embarrassing questions, but the vast majority were reasonable, honest questions by young people desperate to know. In accepting every question, we were able to teach the kids godly behavior. Many times we were thanked for allowing the chance to ask. You'll never believe the misconceptions until you give teenagers a chance to ask.

Sex is not the only topic that a question box may address. We often put out a "Q Box," as it has become known, for Bible study. Some kids do not feel comfortable in admitting what they do not know. It is part of their culture to be "know-it-alls." Honest answers to honest, and maybe a few dishonest, questions is a powerful assistant to any lesson.

Expert panel. Mentioned above under speakers was the use of a panel to address a topic under study. However, those folks may not have been experts.

Expert panels are useful when the topic is specialized or unique. Studying obedience or law and freedom? Ask some Christian police, a judge, and a truant officer in the area to come. Studying Acts? A panel of local missionaries can make the journeys of the Apostles seem more alive.

The great thing about panel discussions is that often the panel guests may disagree on some fine point and display for the kids how Christians can resolve differences of opinion. Also important and obvious in panel discussions is the different directions God may lead us in service to Christ.

One group of missionaries impressed Mark as they spoke of the various ways God called them into the mission field. Some followed a personal call; some found missions the best way to help others; some took a job that became a mission. They each followed a different means to fulfill their ministry calling.

Lesson into series. Sometimes a lesson can spark such interest on a related topic that it is obvious more teaching is needed. Why not turn the lesson into a mini-series that meets apart from the Sunday School time? It can be an elective for those interested.

Recently our group was looking at prayer and some of our girls expressed interest in more study. We held a four week prayer workshop on a different night for those interested in the additional knowledge.

Devil's advocate. Mark loves to shake the kids up and take the non-Christian position on a topic. This works well either by saying, "Just suppose..." and then lunging into the opposite position from that found in Scripture, or by simply asking the adversarial questions. Either way the kids have an opportunity to test what they have learned.

It is important for teenagers to exercise their growth. If unchallenged in their thinking, they will "parrot" the standard answers they have heard all along. They need the challenge such questions bring. A challenge makes them apply what they believe, and it can often reveal the areas in which they feel uncertainty.

Always finish by giving the biblical position and answering the questions which may rise. It also provides a learning moment to describe that our enemy does exactly this in our own times of temptation. Playing the devil's advocate, when done within appropriate limits and not pushed to extremes, lets the high schooler recognize the face and manner of evil. Better she or he face it under your guidance than through a surprising encounter in school or in another less supportive environment.

Practical Application of Adaptation

Enough of the words and descriptions! Let's look at some real life lessons which used adaptations, such as the above, to change lives and encourage spiritual growth.

A Worship Service Dealing With Attempted Suicide

A popular young woman attempted suicide and was unsuccessful. Although not part of our church, she was very well known among our high schoolers. Her attempt came as we were finishing the planning and practicing of our annual Youth Sunday. The kids needed to talk about the unsettling event but also needed to complete and lead a meaningful worship service. To accomplish both needs, we decided to integrate the news and effects of the attempted suicide into our worship service.

Before the call to worship, one teenage girl, who happened to be the best friend of the girl who tried to kill herself, made a statement to the congregation that the service was dedicated to the healing of the young woman. In tears, she called us all to prayer and support of the family. Our chorus selections proclaimed life in Christ. The Scripture selected reflected hope and courage to live in confusing times. Six teenagers delivered sermons with many referring to how the potential death of a good friend impacted them. And so on.

This service was said to be the most significant youth service in our church's memory. Adults were touched; kids shared what was immediate; God was glorified, and His truth applied in the whole process. Multi-level handling of a relevant, serious, and timely event helped the kids to talk about their fears and hurts.

Softball Discrimination and a Christian Sister's Need

In a Sunday School class, some of our girls were looking at the needs, responsibilities, and challenges of Christian friendships. While this was going on, one of the active, but less popular girls, Amanda, was being chided and ridiculed by the junior and senior members of the school softball team. Amanda was taller than the rest of the team so they made fun of her height. She was not the best player, making some errors, and the other girls continually pointed these out. The problems grew as the girls began shoving, hitting, and destroying Amanda's property. Rumors were spread that she was a lesbian. The coach did nothing when this was brought to his attention. The parents of the upper class girls thought it funny.

The Sunday School teacher was at a loss as to how she might integrate the two subjects, Christian friendships and Amanda's dilemma, into a helpful class without making an example of Amanda. She believed that the girls in the class who also played on the team, or knew of it, were being silent because they didn't know what to say, not because they were poor friends.

Aware of the wonderful learning possibilities, she began adding to the Sunday curriculum studies by occasionally playing Devil's Advocate and incorporating spontaneous role playing with skits (drama). She came to class with some Anticipated Q and A's ready for the girls as they looked in God's Word. Bible verses on how Jesus handled conflict were studied. She also had a speaker share some conflict resolution skills ideas that were used in her company when disputes arose.

A couple of days following the completion of the unit, this teacher happened to attend a softball practice and, sure enough, the older girls began attacking Amanda. This time, however, as Amanda burst into tears and began to leave, one of her classmates from Sunday School stood against the "gang" and said, "No more."

Other girls from the class joined in. Another put her arm around Amanda's shoulder. That day, as young Christian women applied the truths learned in church, the abuse stopped. The Sunday School teacher's eyes filled with tears of joy as her heart filled with thanksgiving to God. Amanda was never bothered again.

In these two examples, note that, while the action was accomplished by the high school students, the initiation and adaptation came from the teachers and leaders who *knew their students, were involved in their lives, and who took a situation and adapted the regular lessons into something tailor-made.*

They took the lessons the next step to real life-changing actions, not just more "head knowledge." They were teachers, just like you, who expanded Christian education into daily living.

Current Events
Never be afraid to look at current world events from a biblical perspective. Your students

wonder, even if they do not ask, where is God when events like the Oklahoma City bombings, the Waco inferno, massive hurricane/tornado destruction, oil spills and widespread endorsement of abortion occur. Kids often ask "how can God let this happen?" This is an important time when biblical truths such as the two natures, free will behavior, a fallen world, sin, consequences, and forgiveness can be taught.

One approach is to give each teenager a large piece of posterboard and supply markers, magazines or newspapers, and glue. Have them divide the sheet in two sides and let them make a visual display of the action, the warring natures, and the consequences. Have students ask themselves questions about what led up to the action and search for Bible verses that answer those questions.

For instance, Susan Smith, who murdered her two children, had opportunities to change her mind prior to killing her children. She did not and, instead, entered a cycle of denial, seeing herself as a victim, and then the murders. But what could have happened? Why do people turn away from God? Could God forgive her? How could she have trusted God and changed this outcome in her life?

Or, devise a play with two endings. List various high-profile murders on a piece of paper. Ask the kids to share their opinions on the outcomes as administered by the courts. Then ask them to dig into the Bible to see what Jesus said about murder, about how we should treat others, and about sin.

Assign two groups to write two potentially different endings to these events. One group looks at the human responses as jury members who are deliberating for a verdict. The second writes an ending using Christ's standards of love, forgiveness, and justice.

World events give you the opportunity to examine real-world issues of how fallen human nature sins, Satan's role in the world, and how God responds. The in-depth Bible study as you guide students to the Bible's answers will help them see that God's Word is applicable in every event. God's ways are higher than our ways and often tough to understand.

Bringing these kinds of events into the youth group setting, opening up God's Word, and digging out God's truths for living as well as the consequences of sin, help teens internalize that being a Christian in this culture is no easy task. Such issues are important in assisting the teenagers to clarify their thinking by understanding what the sinful nature is capable of, why refusing to give in to what the sinful nature may want to do is God's way, and how to replace old responses with Christ-like faith.

When discussing tornadoes, terrorism, corporate corruption which compromises human safety for money, oil spills and all the rest, you can teach truths in authentically life-related situations. Emphasize that God is always in control. He is sovereign. But He does not always keep disasters from happening. Jesus wants us to depend on Him and respond to our calls for help.

God doesn't always protect us from the difficulties of life. Teens need to know that. Christians are *in* the world. We are subject to the same condemnation God gave in the Garden of Eden. But we have a Helper who is ready to pull us above the darkness Satan would have people see and show us the light that exists above the clouds. It is our faith that makes a difference in the world to those around us. The church is God's hand in this lost and hurting world. God is always present in profound, helpful ways through His people.

Such issues provide incomparable teaching opportunities for many truths such as God's sovereignty, faith, materialism, our responsibilities to be good stewards, our willingness to make a difference in God's world, the difference salvation makes in our lives.

Adapting topics can accomplish deeper learning. Be yourself, but be willing to move beyond your personal comfort zones and into some new areas of sharing the faith. Mixing it up keeps the class interesting and exciting—always a plus with today's youth.

A word of caution—don't feel it necessary to adapt every session, every week. Plan supplemental activities that make sense and truly draw your students into a deeper understanding. Use these issues as youth group Bible studies and discussions rather than Sunday morning topics.

Curriculum gives the teacher a structured plan to teach biblical truth to students in age-appropriate language and activities. The goals and activities built into the lesson reinforce those truths. These additional ways to customize the lesson are tools that will let you adapt for special situations and needs which are unique to your students.

12 What's Your Teaching Style?

Recently Mark overheard three high school girls comparing their feelings concerning their teachers at school. The girls were very close friends and often shared the same views on many issues. Mark was quite surprised that they could not agree on which teachers were very good, which were all right, and which needed to stock shelves at the hardware store rather than teach.

As the conversation continued, Mark became aware that their evaluation was based on how much of what the teacher said made sense to each individual girl. Basically, the girls had the same needs, problems, likes, experiences, and life styles. However, their learning styles made it impossible for them to agree on which teachers made learning fun for them. As Christian educators we need to realize that it is the same with us as our kids evaluate our teaching.

Just as each student has different learning styles, each teacher communicates information using an equally different style. In general, our learning styles are closely linked to our teaching styles. Most teachers automatically default in their teaching to the characteristics which fit their learning styles.

For instance...Mark is a *dynamic learner* with some considerable *imaginative learner* characteristics. He is highly visual. Kathy is highly *imaginative* with strong influences in *analytic and common sense* learning styles. She is kinesthetic. While Mark enjoys noise, talking, and flair, Kathy would rather work quietly in an orderly area and alone.

Mark loves to get in front of high schoolers to share, teach, or just goof around. Kathy enjoys a classroom full of students, but thrives on the stories and experiences of each individual student.

Mark would rather take the whole youth group to a concert or a museum. Kathy likes it better when she and one or two others enjoy the event.

Both of us tend to let ideas "brew" or "percolate," but Kathy is much more likely to brew for a longer time while Mark will jump it more swiftly—sometimes with less than perfect results. Both of us are educated and like to research and develop ideas or materials, but Kathy thrives on cross-referencing studies and resources to formulate the best, most concise and exhaustive presentation possible while Mark will hit a limit and be satisfied.

We both speak to groups, but Mark is more entertaining, comfortable and engaging in his presentations. Kathy writes in a very business-like manner; Mark with more imagination and verve. And so it goes. We tend to teach in the ways we learn—which is certainly accurate in our cases.

There is nothing wrong with teaching from our personal learning styles. We are who we are. However, when any of us get locked into our style of teaching with no consideration to those with differing styles, then we can count on minimizing the potential learning in our classrooms.

Teenagers will learn from us if: a) they are the same style of learners as we are, b) we are dealing with a topic of great interest to them, or c) we have bribed them! In other words, to be the most effective, we have to adapt our teaching/learning styles rather than try to force the students to learn in our comfort zone. We must involve other styles by incorporating elements and approaches of the other styles. This is inexpensive insurance for effective teaching.

For example, John, a Sunday School teaching friend of ours, loves discussion and the give and take of dissecting a topic using each person's views and opinions. He is a favorite among high school students because he lets them talk, too. Kids at this age love to put in their 2 cents and find few forums which allow them to present their opinions. So, John's class is animated and exciting for a few weeks, then attendance or interest drops off.

First the *analytic learners* begin to drop out, either physically or mentally. As long as the opinion driven debates eventually get to the point of a correct answer, they will hang in there to be with their friends. But if some concrete answers or conclusions are not forthcoming before the class ends, they check out.

Next the *common sense learners* become disinterested. Opinions are good and revealing, and they like to hear various positions of a problem, but what they want is the "how-to" end of the discussion for a solution.

The *dynamic learner* will like the creative nature of the discussion and are curious, but they need some creative expression and can't take the same format three weeks in a row.

Imaginative learners stay the longest because they love to listen and to talk about ideas. They tend to learn through talking.

However, discussion-only classes never quite seem to get to the facts of what *God's Word* teaches on the subject. The issues never get settled and much is left "up for grabs." All of these kids need for John to conclude with a value; a bottom line. They need to hear what the Bible says as the definitive answer or guidance along the path. They may agree; they may disagree, but they need an adult to bring some level of summation to the discussion.

The same scenario applies to the teacher who attempts to communicate through too many craft or symbolic lessons. Or the teacher who brings in a truck load of resource materials and assigns some learning project using books with a "discover the answer for yourself" direction.

In fact, any mode of teaching that is done for three or four weeks in a row will trip the "Been there - Done that" switch that is so much a part of today's youth culture.

There is not one good reason for a teen to be bored in Sunday School. Even resistant learners can be hooked somehow. We must look for ways to adapt ourselves so that the learning channels are not blocked.

However, a warning must be offered for the other extreme of trying too many varieties of learning, too often. Some balance and predictability is desirable. When each week becomes an event or seems to compete with whatever was done last week, then learning becomes secondary to the production. Your influence as teacher risks being abandoned for the role of entertainer.

Interestingly, many churches seem to be moving toward this type of worship service leaving many in the congregations feeling, "What's wrong with just going to church to worship God?" We can teach Christ's gospel without going Madison Avenue or concert hall. Jesus certainly "mixed it up" in His teaching methods, but never at the expense of the lesson. The truth He taught was always paramount, always clear.

Identifying Your Teaching Style

Learning who we are, as teachers, is something we discover, not something that we just know. Often our assumption is that all teachers are similar to us. We figure that what we do is done the same by everyone. However, even a simple stroll through the various classes in your church will cement the certainty that teachers are not peas in a pod. We have differing gifts and abilities—no argument there—but we also have different styles revealed in our numerous approaches. It is a marvelous example of God's love of variety.

The following is an overview of some of the characteristics and qualities of the different learning styles. A look at learning styles will reflect what kinds of activities and approaches we will tend to use in our teaching. We strongly feel that learning styles give us the keys to knowing our teaching styles.

Read each of the four categories and check mark in pencil the items which seem to describe you. One will likely be weighted more heavily than the others. In fact, one style should find you marking almost every line. This is your primary learning style and will be your primary teaching style. We recommend that a friend or spouse review your check marks to offer you some personalized reflection on what you have discovered. It can be very affirming to hear others tell us of our gifts.

When you finish checking the items, take a piece of paper and develop a personal description of your styles and approaches. Your individual style will be an accumulation of all of your approaches. Make this to be a fun exercise and do not let criticism distract you! You are the person God created, so learn to love it. Just because another style seems more flashy or upbeat is not to presume it is in any way a better style. Nothing could be further from the truth. Our high schoolers need all of us in all of our various styles. Be true to who God has created you to be.

The Imaginative teacher will:
❑ tend to give overviews and speak expansively

- ❏ love distributing lots of ideas
- ❏ think in terms of "Why?" or "Why not?"
- ❏ be very friendly and easy to like
- ❏ have lots of ideas for projects or lessons
- ❏ not be upset if things get noisy
- ❏ love to talk and share
- ❏ know how to listen attentively
- ❏ avoid lectures or long speeches
- ❏ not like working alone
- ❏ tend to be good judges of personality
- ❏ be more feeling oriented than thinking oriented
- ❏ be people persons
- ❏ love to role play or make the lesson an act
- ❏ avoid making anyone win or lose
- ❏ be there for the kids and not so concerned about test-like evaluations
- ❏ want to decorate the room and sit in non-typical arrangements
- ❏ make the class a group and avoid too much individuality
- ❏ be each student's friend
- ❏ will learn as they talk about the lesson

These teachers are driven by how a class feels and will be sensitive to the students. They sometimes seem disorganized and can tend to shoot from the hip. They are often popular due to their friendliness and carefree ways. Their rooms are very busy, both in the work of the class and any decorating. While teaching a Bible lesson is important to them, what is more important is how the class is doing.

The Analytic teacher will:
- ❏ love to share information and facts
- ❏ teach lessons in order, not skip around
- ❏ approach lessons with logic and rationality
- ❏ teach in terms of right and wrong
- ❏ be tempted to debate a topic
- ❏ come off as being intellectual
- ❏ have plenty of notes about a lesson
- ❏ love to give out plenty of information and facts
- ❏ not enjoy a noisy or active classroom
- ❏ tend to teach in traditional fashions
- ❏ be drawn to students who seem to be smart or well informed
- ❏ look for the principles of the lesson
- ❏ seem disinterested or impersonal
- ❏ seem somewhat competitive or driven

These teachers may seem to be boring or uninspired due to their lecture-and-fact style. They often have keen minds and can figure out almost any problem. Their classrooms are usually neat and orderly with class held in a discussion circle or around tables. They like hand outs and may instruct the class on finding answers in Bible dictionaries or other research works. They may seem cold or impersonal on the surface and like to give particular verses as answers to high schoolers' problems.

The Common Sense teacher will:
- ❏ constantly want to be in motion as they teach
- ❏ love to assist in helping students recognize how to live a lesson

161

❑ have a goal in mind
❑ incorporate skills and abilities into the lesson
❑ be able to talk about consequences
❑ avoid the lecture format
❑ evaluate success by how well a project proceeds
❑ do well in problem solving with the "how-to" approach
❑ love to demonstrate a lesson
❑ be driven by action
❑ be likely to link the learning of the classroom with some mission activity

These teachers will value the project over the "touchy-feely" part of a lesson. They love to get things done, often doing it themselves to be sure it is done right. They can take on any project and would rather do it than talk about it. Their classrooms may have lots of projects or symbols which represent faith in action. The Bible is a motivational tool for action. They are not quiet and avoid pencil and paper learning.

The Dynamic teacher will:
❑ have a good sense of humor and can be entertaining
❑ lead the students into learning for themselves
❑ enjoy creative ways of teaching the lesson
❑ be known as "people persons"
❑ be intuitive
❑ have good communications skills and be comfortable in front of the students
❑ not want to do things as they have always been done before

❑ want lessons that have alternatives
❑ facilitate problem-solving or issues from various directions
❑ take the risks needed to be interesting
❑ tend to be dramatic or teach with flair
❑ need a flexible space in which to teach
❑ not seem as efficient as other teachers may appear
❑ involve the students in every aspect of learning
❑ let the class "take over" if they can do so appropriately
❑ want artistic options to teaching a lesson
❑ sometimes want to teach in an unused part of the church instead of their room

These teachers are full of zip and ideas. They sometimes feel constrained by the curriculum and often feel the need to go off in other directions. Classrooms seem restrictive, at times, and they may wish to hold class in a chapel or the boiler room. They are competent communicators and can hold attention. Give them an idea and they will take off and run with it. Even if unsuccessful, they will try new approaches for the value of the option and find some way to bring some successful conclusion to the experiment.

Which teacher are you? Or, more accurately, which styles blend to make you the special teacher you truly are? We hope you have gained some insight into your dominant style.

Equally important is to recognize the other styles which are not as dominant in your teaching nor as prevalent in your approaches to a lesson. Just as each classroom has different styles of students, it is not a matter of choice to learn of other approaches. You must to be effective. Brainstorm some ways you might learn to incorporate other teaching styles into your classroom. This insures that each high schooler will get her or his learning avenues met.

An interesting and helpful exercise that your church Sunday School Superintendent may wish to offer sometime would be to look at a number of lessons in your high school curriculum from each of the various teaching styles. As this is important to any teacher in any grade, we would recommend your teacher fellowship gather with this in mind and develop a program in which four teachers share how they would teach a lesson drawing solely on their dominant, personal style. Of course, it would be best to ask teachers who truly represent each of the four styles to simply be themselves.

This is a great insight builder for all of the teachers. Often we have observed that the freer teaching styles receive some criticism for being too expansive, while the more lecture-based styles are denounced for being boring. This is not a matter of who is right or wrong, better or worse. Make it a celebration of the varieties God has blessed us with in pursuit of all being the best they can possibly be. Challenge each teacher to take the same lesson and try to teach it solely from another style, then incorporate all of the learning styles in the same lesson.

Experienced teachers know that teaching is a process of becoming. Do not fear trying to expand your style because with a bit of information, example, and help, you can do it as well as the next teacher. Never apologize for who you are, but, equally important, never avoid becoming more than you currently are.

In our daily lives, we all strive to become more like Jesus. In our classrooms, the goal is the same. Jesus displayed a remarkable variety of teaching and communication skills. As encouragement and example to us, let's look at some of His approaches and insights.

13 *Learning From Jesus' Teaching Style*

Have you studied Christ's teaching styles? As teachers of high schoolers, we can draw amazing and applicable lessons from Christ's communication styles. He met us on every level of our lives, making God's truths accessible to the faithful. He touched lives by being real and sincere, never making any feel inadequate.

For many of our teenagers, you will be the person through whom the gospel is made real. If Christ is making a difference in your life, the young people will begin to believe that it can happen for them, also. They are struggling with their faith values and the examples set by their parents, teachers, and other Christians. They want to believe and find their own personal faith, but they are actively questioning and challenging everything. You, an adult they love, respect, and trust, can be the real world example they need to accept what they know in their heart is true.

Jesus' life and ministry can be our example and model of the life lived for God. To borrow from His ministry is to emulate our Master, improve our teaching, and impact the lives we touch.

A word of caution before we look at Christ's ministry tools. Only imitate what works for you.

Imitation takes practice. The tools must be part of your personal styles of learning and teaching, your own personality and abilities. Play with these suggestions in your mind and try them on the kids. It's OK to stumble and sort through the various tools described. They can only enhance what you accomplish with your classes.

Let's look at some of Jesus' ministry styles. Jesus used these as the natural overflow of who He was, and is, in God.

■ **Jesus understood relevance to daily living.** He knew how important it was to make the lessons fit the daily experiences of His listeners.

To overlook that would be to trivialize their existence. To make these occurrences a natural part of His examples validated their loves as important and valuable.

So, Jesus spoke of crops and farmers, of common animals, of humans in trouble or disagreement. He made a point to discuss the problems of religious leaders who did not concern themselves with God's people. To people under Roman occupation, He spoke of conflict and true freedom. All of these examples underlined what the people knew and lived. They were real-life application.

How does this apply in your classes? You might relate a lesson topic to the sense of isolation that teenagers today experience. Or to specific examples of the battles they face with sex, drugs, gangs, and obeying parents, temptation to steal, etc. Use recognizable things like technology, cars, airplanes, first dates, graduation, settling arguments, divorce, or AIDS to bring a lesson home to their hearts.

This interjects the Good News into their world in a way that can only strengthen their understanding of the relevance of what God is teaching them through His Word.

■ **Ministering from within the group.** Jesus knew very well that He was an outsider to the religious establishment of His day. Although some called Him Rabbi, or teacher, His way was not the orthodox, accepted way of the religious leaders.

However, Jesus was one of the common people of His day. He walked among the poor and needy. He talked and ate with the outcasts, both impoverished and unpopular, like the woman at the well, the lepers, and the tax collectors. He drew the majority of His followers from those of His day who were seen as the commoners and insignificant. In His association with all people, He made His greatest advances.

Teenagers do not want you to become one of them. They do, however, want you to be with them, to know their confusion, to understand their struggles. Significant ministry is accomplished through attending their sporting events, their school plays, by celebrating their personal achievements. Being with them means remembering their needs, praying for them, and then telling them you did so. They need to know that you care about what they face.

To minister among them is to extend to them the promise that you believe they are important and special, both to you and to God. It tells them you are real and in their corner.

■ **Using real-life common examples.** Jesus was a master at making a true life example an illustration for the spiritual side of life. He could discuss God's love by noting how well God cares for birds and flowers, and then comparing this care to great spiritual leaders of historic Judaism as he did with Solomon.

Teenagers have busy, complicated lives. Using challenges from their daily living will go far in helping them make application of spiritual principles to their own walk with Christ.

Often we become frustrated because we know this stuff and they seem unaware of it. Truth is, they often do not know until we tell them. Much of what we teach them is foreign and new to them.

We know of a young convert who was quite active sexually. When he accepted Christ, no one told him that this behavior was wrong. He continued to seek women as "conquests." Finally, someone pulled him aside and questioned him. In shock, he confessed that having absolutely no prior Christian experience, he was unaware that his actions were sin. He ceased immediately. Lesson: He did not know until someone told him. After learning, he was able to relate real-life examples to biblical truth about sexual immorality.

■ **Making God understandable and reachable.** Sometimes in our awe and respect for God, we make Him a bit untouchable. Jesus spoke of God very personally and with great familiarity. He spoke of God, His Father. He told everyone He met that a personal relationship with God was possible and revealed that God's passion for us was unimaginable.

God is often presented as being too great, too big, and too busy to bother with our petty needs. Access to God doesn't seem realistic. He's just too busy with the affairs of the universe to be pestered with our insignificant requests.

These fears plague our teenagers today. Recently, a high school sophomore asked Mark if we could pray about her grandfather's operation. She preceded the request with a disclaimer that she figured God was too busy or that it was a silly request, but could we anyway. Although his heart was saddened by her feeling that she needed to screen her prayer requests, he used the moment to assure the teenagers that God is never too busy for our prayers and loves to hear from us. A number of the teenagers felt noticeably better after hearing this.

Teens need to be reassured that God loves them as they are and for who they will become in Him.

■ **Concerns for the simple and disadvantaged.** At a soup kitchen our senior high youth operate monthly, the question came up as to how God could abandon these people who were so poor and so disadvantaged. The response was that, just as Jesus made it His business to help the needy, so were we on the last Sunday of every month. We assured the teenagers that God was here and showing his concern through our actions and hot food.

We go as Christians into the inner city of one of Cleveland's most desperate neighborhoods and feed the hungry. We play with the children and sometimes bring gifts. We sit and eat with the adults, sharing companionship together, not just serving them.

Teenagers are concerned about the injustices in the world. They need to know that wealth is not an ironclad affirmation of God's presence, and poverty is not an indication that God has abandoned us. Jesus lived in the midst of inequities and wrongs, and He sends us to stand for Him in our world today. His example becomes our encouragement to do as He did, and would do if He walked among us today.

■ **The power of compassionate touch.** Jesus touched those to whom He ministered. He offered his hand of love to the shoulders of the needy. He held the children and touched lepers. He confirmed His love with an appropriate touch.

In spite of the abuses and horror stories of people who touch in wrong ways, we need to confirm our love and acceptance by knowing when to offer the right kind of touch. Be aware and be smart. Don't hug a teenager when alone. Don't put yourself in places where misunderstanding might develop.

We always greet with handshakes or pats on the back. We close our meetings with prayer circles where we hold hands. There are many ways to touch that underline our love and presence. Touch in good ways.

■ **The Parable.** Jesus spoke of the world around Him in stories that brought home the spiritual truths He sought to communicate.

His parables have been called, "earthly stories with heavenly meanings." They are teaching tools which use the real world and real situations to enhance the spiritual truth of a message.

Browse the many parables you know so well. The meanings are plain and easy to grasp. The lessons bring sights and sounds and textures to mind which reinforce the meaning. Jesus spoke of a farmer casting his seed in hopes of a successful planting and bountiful harvest. He talked of seed falling on hard, dry paths, on rocks and onto good ground. Just try to stop the images which flood your mind as you read or listen to Christ's parables.

That is why they work so well—for Jesus and for us. At almost any age the pictures of the parables relate to daily living and human experience. Even a child can grasp them on some level. The pictures stick in our minds and can be replayed over and over.

Teach with parables from today's experiences. Add pictures to your lessons which use the physical world to communicate heavenly and spiritual principles.

Recently, we heard a speaker use a football story to teach about discipleship and Christian caring and support. Athletes listened. Spectators listened. Band members listened. Even sports haters listened. They could each relate to the sermon because the speaker used a common, understandable example to illustrate the lessons.

■ **The Ridiculous.** Jesus knew we, as humans, could be ridiculous in our doings. He liked to use our goofy doings to help us see our inconsistencies and contradictions. Let's face it, fishing for tax money and stating that the coin should be given to the person whose face was upon the coin is pretty strange. Yet, the lesson obvious.

■ **Serious examination of Scripture.** Jesus was not afraid to tackle faulty understandings of the Jewish Law as a teaching tool for those in His day. It was not that the Scripture was wrong, but the religious leaders in His day were using bad interpretations to manipulate the people. They used God's Word to control and dominate. A good example of this is Christ's treatment of healing on the Sabbath in Matthew 12:8-13.

We may need to seriously examine the Scriptures with our teenagers to help them see how the Bible is used by some for personal gains. As a teenager in the Civil Rights years of the 1960s, Mark sometimes saw the Bible misused to defend racism and hatred. History shows that it was used around the time of the Civil War to defend slavery. When such abuses occur, it is very redeeming to examine the Word closely with our young adults to see what God is really saying. Teenagers often reject God's Word because they don't understand it and can't look up the true position of Scripture for themselves. They feel unqualified to check it out. As leaders, we can help them in their search for truth by opening the Bible with them in search of what is really being said.

■ **Example.** Jesus is said to be the only founder of a faith who actually lived His teachings. He practiced what He preached. His world could not dispute His claims using the example of His life. His life, His actions, and His words consistently proved He was the Son of God.

The teenagers in your youth group are watching you and listening to each word for inconsistencies. It may seem like they are just waiting for you to fail. In actuality, they are waiting to see if you succeed using your faith as your guide. Make a mistake and expect them to they nail you. If you are successful, expect them to be silent. But never doubt that they are watching and learning.

Living your faith is a great encouragement to high schoolers. How you handle fears, disappointments, success, financial setbacks, injustice, pride are all stored inside their minds. It helps them to see that the claims of our faith in Christ are livable, reasonable, and possible. Faith becomes a support and not a crutch; an answer and not an excuse. It gives them hope and direction.

■ **Modeling.** Similar to example, modeling is actively and intentionally "going through the motions" of what a faith-filled life is truly about.

Jesus modeled prayer through the Lord's Prayer. He modeled humility and service by washing the feet of His disciples. All the words in the world will not equal the impact of your actions.

Ever watch a parent trying to teach a child to eat from a spoon for the first time? Usually, they put food on the spoon and pretend to eat it themselves. They do this over and over, often for many meals, to illustrate to the toddler how it is done. Eventually, the child gets the idea and eats from a spoon by herself. That's modeling.

■ **Mentoring.** Jesus lived His faith before the masses each time He taught. However, He also drew aside with His 12 disciples and communicated the finer points of faith with them in a small group setting. He knew that He would not be with them forever. So, He invested heavily in their personal internalization of truth so that they might lead when He was gone. He practiced discipleship, or the making of disciples by careful and close interaction and instruction. He tutored them in the faith which He also modeled for them.

Today, this practice is often called mentoring. At the turn of the century it was the apprenticeship approach to teaching a trade to a novice. Whatever it is called, it is a wonderful means to pass the faith on. It offers the learner an opportunity to interact with the lesson and to experience a deeper understanding under the guidance of the teacher.

Teenagers love this relationship. It is the small group Bible study or the Leadership Team. It is the one-on-one conversation over a soda. It is time spent with only a few, based on a relationship of mutual love and respect. It is one of the very best ways to pass on faith.

■ **Reality-Based.** Of great importance to teenagers today is the presentation of on-going growth in Christ as reality-based. They don't want theory or what you tell them something *should* be.

Reality-based teaching is often used to describe education that is relevant to the world as it is today. It seeks to bestow upon the learner a better understanding of how faith can be applied in today's world. Many teens hear teachers and other authority figures make the claim that faith is totally irrelevant to the world we live in. They say faith is outdated. They question the function of faith in a secular culture.

It's no wonder our teens are confused. They hear two voices. Which one influences their lives is, in some part, dependent upon you.

Life has not changed much since the beginning of human history. There will always be skeptics who want to ridicule faith or eliminate it. Yet, we know, as mature Christians, that there is more to life than the tangible and physical. Teens, however, are just leaving the realm of concrete thinking. They have not yet had time to discover this truth.

Reality-based faith living does not deny the power of God, even though it is invisible and intangible. Kids are looking for faith that functions; that works for them in school, at home, and in their activities. They are seeking real answers to a pretty "up for grabs" world. Reality-based faith provides these answers.

■ **Unencumbered by complexity.** A favorite sermon story is that of a pastor who received a note on his pulpit from his wife with the letters K. I. S. S. He preached his sermon with great vigor as he interpreted the note to mean his wife wanted a kiss. At home he asked her the meaning, believing he already knew. She told him that she had had it with his intellectual and overly academic sermons and put the note there to remind him to "Keep it simple, stupid."

While the pastor probably did not appreciate being called stupid, we can all remember to share the simple gospel of God's love for all. It is easy to fall into the trap that knowledge holds for us. First Corinthians 8:1 tells us that, "Knowledge puffeth up." It has a way of making us feel superior or more important.

Jesus knew it all, inside and out. Yet, He never used His knowledge to complicate His message. He let the second part of that truth in I Corinthians dominate, "charity edifieth." He resisted the complex to make understanding easier so that would reap benefits in every hearer's life. His applications were equally simple.

Teenagers hunger for simplicity and clarity in the teaching of the Word. They have lives of complexity and fast-paced expectation. They are called upon to excel and achieve. What they need is some time to reflect. Giving them a simple faith does not deprive them of its importance. It assures them that God is not watching just to make sure they jump through the proper hoops.

■ **Satisfied with those given Him.** Although Jesus continually sought to share His message with the lost, He was committed to those God had given Him (John 17:6-24).

We live in a numbers-oriented society and, all too often, overlook what God has already given us in hopes of adding more.

At one point, Mark bought into this mentality and would weekly encourage the kids to gather up the slackers and bring in new kids. Finally, one wise young woman suggested that we forget the others who never came and make sure we worked with the ones who were committed to the group each week. It was humbling, but he heeded her wisdom.

It is a ministry fact that we can only build with those we have. We cannot use those not coming, so we need to attend to the wonderful teenagers God has brought to our groups. Sure, we need to continue sharing the Word to the lost, but not to the exclusion of those already coming for spiritual development and growth.

■ **Unimpressed by power, stature, position.** Jesus sat with the tax collector, the infirm, the hated and often ignored the lofty, the secure, and the powerful. He had no regard for worldly achievement. He was not impressed by lengthy resumes or honors banquets. He had come for all who would believe in Him, not those who only wanted to argue.

We need to monitor our own favoritism, making sure we accept and respect each teen. Teenagers wilt when we pay attention to the best looking, the most athletic, or the most gifted. We need to make sure we don't have "teacher's pets."

■ **Immediate and accessible.** Jesus was there for His followers and usually for the seekers who flocked to Him. His ministry was focused on the moment but always within the context of how it led into eternity, be it understanding God, taxes, politics, healing, or greater spiritual awareness. He was rarely short-tempered with those surrounding Him. Jesus was immediate and accessible.

It is important that we be likewise. Teenagers today feel little connection with most adults. They often do not trust us. Granted, this is their perception, however, we have to meet them within their point of view. Once accepted, we can help to change it.

Kids will need you according to their schedules. Two a.m. phone calls are not unusual. Inconvenient dropping in is not unheard of. It is important to set appropriate limits in consideration of your family and other responsibilities. Yet, do so with grace, aware that the teaching moment or the time of needed assistance is crucial to their lives and spiritual growth. Let them know when you can always be sought out, as well as how they can get to you when they have need.

Jesus was the most remarkable Human to ever walk among this earth. We can never measure up to His character. We can, however, take note of His ministry skill and endeavor to match our styles to His. He was our example.

In Acts we see the name "Christian" used for the first time. It means "little Christ" and was used to refer to the church's dependency on, and faith in, its Savior. The name stuck because it was not seen as a negative. It was perceived as a good way to describe early believers.

Our goal is to be like Jesus. To reach out beyond ourselves into the lives of the lost, hurting and needy. We are "little Christs" in all of the good meanings, recognizing the source of our life and faith. Jesus shows the way for us to be loving and caring, that we might lead the way for our youth.

14 *Pulling It All Together*

We are nearly done with our journey, and what a journey it has been! We have run the length and breadth of church ministry to today's teenagers, carefully examining their world.

Think about where we have gone. We have noted it is a changing world for teenagers and discussed that while it is no big news to us, changes are still "firsts" to them. We have learned to adapt, but we sometimes forget that this is the first trip around that block for them.

We have examined how they are developing on many levels. We have seen who these kids are in our classrooms and noted some statistical factors which are involved in their lives. We have looked at needs, ours and theirs, with a discussion of specifics that we, and they, may receive from one another. We have sought to better understand the art of teaching, exploring learning styles and differences, with some thoughts concerning disabilities.

Finally, we looked at some ways we can enhance our teaching of high schoolers by adapting the topics found in our lesson plans to specific needs in their lives.

We all approach the privilege of teaching these budding young adults a bit thunderstruck and astounded, but we can all learn. The Holy Spirit is our Comforter and Helper. The secret is to be prepared in advance and to "hang loose" enough that the teaching moment may be fully utilized.

In interviewing potential senior high youth leaders and teachers, we have seen some consistent fears and feelings from those determining if youth ministry is for them. Often they ask these questions.

- Can I do it?
- Will the kids like me?
- Will I be trained?
- Can I bridge the age differences?
- Am I spiritually mature enough?
- How will I handle the tough questions?
- What if I mess up a lesson?
- What if I fail and the group doesn't grow?

So, What is Important to Teenagers?

Honing in on their world is the initial step in determining which topics are important to teenagers in your high school classes. A connection needs to be consciously made between what is important to them and what you need to do to teach God's Word. Just saying you can relate to their fears about drugs or relationships or family problems is not going to etch you a place in their hearts. However, if you share some of your stories concerning these issues, and listen to their stories without lecturing them, correcting them, or attempting "one-upsmanship" in which your story is better than theirs, you'll go a long way in showing them you are a safe, understanding adult committed to working *with* them and not *for* them.

Usually, their concerns fall into two basic categories. The Personal Issues and the Top Controversies of the Day.

Personal Issues

There are common issues teens face in high school. These either vie for their attention, challenge their faith, confound their thinking, or give their lives meaning and purpose. Some of these are:

The future
Dating and sexual conflicts
Love, marriage, children
Relationships, friendships
Profession, career, money, college
The return of Christ
Health and fitness
Spirituality, pleasing God
How and where they fit in
Parent, family, and sibling concerns
Temptations
Drugs and alcohol
Death, dying and the fear of loved ones deaths
Grades and image, class ranking, teachers' lives
Dress, their personal look, if they are good looking, body image.
Blunders, mistakes, or embarrassing moments

These personal issues comprise the vast majority of their personal prayer concerns and their unspoken prayer requests. Care about these issues and similar others, and you'll earn your place in their hearts.

Top Controversies
These are less personal concerns which, nonetheless, cause them anxiety and merit high consideration.

Homosexuality and AIDS

Abortion

Sexual, domestic, and child abuse

War, violence, terrorism, gangs

Contracting a major illness or debilitating injury

Drug or alcohol abuse in a generic sense

Organized religion, other faiths, cults, occult

Racism, injustice, prejudice, discrimination

The poor, needy, elderly, mourning, injured

Recycling, caring for the planet, pollution

These two categories of concern center in their quest for self-definition and an understanding of who they are becoming. They are thinking about their place in the Big Picture of life and faith. With the over-abundance of information at their fingertips, they cannot discern between which things are essential, which are important, which are interesting, and which are insignificant. There are no filters through which they can view these concerns in proper importance.

That's why you are so important. You become the sounding board, the point of definition, the safe place where they can "let it all hang out."

Some of high school kids have found their churches to be rather disappointing in response to these concerns in their lives. For most churches, the Sunday School program is usually dissected into small classrooms centered around grades. The youth group is a slightly larger accumulation of three or four grade levels. Both are all but separate from the life and work of the rest of the church.

Kids see this and wonder about it. It is part of our job to integrate them into the church body. It is part of our job to remember always that their world is not our world.

As adults we deal with limited incomes, mortgage payments, troubles in raising our own kids, work frustrations, getting older, and all the rest. It is sometimes difficult to be sympathetic when Janey or Joey Youth Group Member is moaning because dad won't be home in time to take them to ball practice so they have to walk nearly eight blocks, or when they fume because mom won't allow them to get a seventh earring. It may be laughable to us, but it's the real world to them. We must realize that there are those in the church who cannot relate to the values and lives of young people—especially junior high and high school kids. But we chose this ministry. The kids have a right to expect us to lead them into appropriate choices and responses which will help them learn how to react or respond to life's more difficult choices.

Beware of letting your Sunday School class become "sensory deadening." Too often we save the "fun" stuff for the activities and retreats. But the high school years are critical "launch pad" years into adulthood. Make the teaching of these years memorable and applicable to their lives.

Teenagers no longer like being referred to as "kids." However, they strongly need and want to retain some of the childhood experiences and behaviors they are growing out of. So, we play "stupid" games, and we laugh and play harmless tricks in youth group and at Sunday School as part of the whole package. And they love it. They come back. They learn that the Bible is true and that God can be trusted with their problems.

High school Christian education must move beyond facts into application. Our lessons should be a synthesis of what has been learned in the past, what life has shown the learner along the way, and what they believe about God. These years should resemble how a chocolate cake mix looks early in the mixing process. Blending together we see the swirl of dark brown powder, the yellow egg, the white milk as they spiral together. In a few seconds the various colors become a single color. That's the process in which you are called as a youth worker.

Classroom Applications of Relevancy

At the risk of being redundant, we would like to address the nature of intentional relevancy in the classroom or teaching setting.

In a teaching setting we often revert to the lecture means of dispensing information. It is how most of us were taught. It is how most of us think teaching is supposed to occur. Yet, it is ineffective when used as the only means. And kids usually stop listening after a few minutes.

Sometimes the lecture format is the only one that can be used due to other constraints. So, does the lesson have to be risked because of the setting? No. In fact, when the lecture is enhanced with other modes of learning, it can be powerful.

For example, your lesson is a study of the Sermon on the Mount in Matthew 5. Some suggestions might be to...

• Ask the kids to close their eyes as you read the Beatitudes to them. Suggest they try to picture what form blessings might take. Ask some to share their thoughts after reading the entire section.

• Recite the Beatitudes by saying the first phrase of each one and having the kids say the second phrase together. This may sound juvenile, yet, they will remember more of the portion if they hear and recite.

• Any musicians in the group? Put the Beatitude section to music. Or establish a rhythm by "drumming" your thighs and recite the portion to the beat.

• Look for symbols or objects that etch the verse in memory, like salt, light, city, or candlestick.

• Ask the students how they might "build" these verses if they had to construct them (Common Sense). Or how these verses might be developed into a mime (Imaginative). Or what values are taught (Analytic). Or how they could be re-written into today's language or situations (Dynamic).

There is little reason for teens to be bored by a lesson. Treating it in non-traditional ways will make it a completely new lesson.

To take it deeper, have each student commit to making one verse real in their lives this week. Get a promise from them that they will try to live the truths of that verse each day. Have them think about the verse that draws them each day. Surprisingly, when high schoolers promise to do something, they often follow through. Even the ones who seem tough to reach. Have them write their selected verse on a 3 x 5 card and carry it with them.

Upon leaving, offer each teenager a candle (to remind them of verse 14) or a packet of salt (verse 13). Tell them that you believe in them and their ability to fulfill Christ's hope for them as salt and light. Having done these kinds of "gimmicky" reminders for years, we are used to the fact that the kids very often hold on to the keepsake, mentioning years later that they still have the candle on their dresser at college or their packet of salt is still in their Bible at Matthew 5. The symbol becomes relevant to their experience in your class and an important benchmark of their spiritual development.

The Largest, Most Biggest, Hugest Relevancy of All

Teaching high schoolers is an art form that can be learned. It is an adventure only for those God calls into this challenging, rewarding place of ministry.

We touch the lives of today's youth at a time when they need direction and clarification. The world has little to offer beyond cheap thrills and learning to overlook what is important. Public education will swell their heads with information, but offers very little in the way of learning the vital lessons for life. Our media is bent on introducing ungodly lifestyles and behaviors to our youth in the name of its brand of what's okay. As values slip and morals plummet, our youth need our influence and love.

So, what is the most important aspect of youth work? What really changes lives and turns head for Christ? How can we meet the needs of our youth and insure that the church will be healthy and evident in tomorrow's world?

By thanking *you* for taking the time to lead and teach the young adults of our churches. You are the most important piece of relevancy that our kids will experience. You live the life of faith. You become the godly model and mentor many will not find elsewhere. With your imperfections, your doubts, your irritations, your problems, our youth may see, first hand, that the best proof of God is how ordinary saints of God live.

You'll make mistakes. You'll embarrass yourself. You may even teach something that is not quite what God intended. And they'll love you and respect you anyway. Why? Because while most of the world criticizes them or belittles them, you are spending time with them. You are investing in their knowledge of God's Word. You are making sure your church doesn't accidentally overlook their needs and their place in God's body. You are making the difference every time you prepare a lesson and take it to them.

It matters not if your class has three kids or 60. It doesn't really matter if you can entertain like a professional comedian or if you are a Bible scholar. Keep in mind Moses' advanced age and speech impediment as he stood for God in front of the most powerful man in his world.

What matters is that you are taking your life in Christ to the classroom to be an example for them. In profound, wonderful ways, you are changing lives for Christ. They will look back and remember you and the time you gave them.

However, in order to remain effective, don't forget to take time for yourself, for your family, for your own spiritual growth. You cannot be an island. You need the church group, the fellowship of other adults, the encouragement of friends. Do you have a personal support group? Do you take time alone to recharge your own inner "batteries"? You must if you are to minister effectively.

May God bless you and your church as you serve young people. We believe that our churches have a much better chance of producing dynamic, spiritual, dedicated servants of God as a result of your unselfish and devoted efforts.

Thank you for all you do.

About the Authors

Teaching Today's Youth is the first joint writing adventure of Mark and Kathy Simone, a dynamic husband/wife team who have been actively involved in church ministry for 22 years.

Mark's work as Youth Minister spans almost two decades. He holds a Masters of Divinity degree in Pastoral Psychology and Counseling. He is also a frequent conference and retreat speaker and has authored numerous youth ministry articles. His first book was *Ministering to Kids Who Don't Fit* (1993).

Kathy works as an art teacher in the public school system. Her previous experience includes work as Christian Education Supervisor. She has also developed Parent Forum programs for the local church. A skilled enamelist and painter, Kathy holds a BFA degree in Crafts and a BS degree in Education

The Simones live in Chagrin Falls, Ohio with their four children.